All Aboard:
Tracks Headed to "Self" City

PACING, PACING, PACING—I felt like a caged animal walking my house in the dead of night, as if my motion could accomplish what I wanted: escape. I wanted to escape my body, my thoughts…everything. I stopped. Standing stock-still, my head dropped back with my face toward the ceiling, and sobs erupted from deep within me. *What am I to do, Lord?* These moments describe the insanity I experienced prior to breaking into the small safe we kept inside my husband's bedroom closet, a safe which no longer held insurance papers or legal documents but my prescription narcotics and marijuana.

The compulsion for my safe-breaking act was a true Dr. Jekyll and Ms. Hyde moment for me. Such reckless and deceptive behavior juxtaposed with the typical restrained emotions, discipline, and diligent behavior required to achieve a doctorate in law or start a law firm, all while juggling married life with kids. How did I get here? Well, I asked the Lord the same question, and writing my memoirs was how I discovered his answer.

My unexpected decline in health lasted years beyond my expectations, stripping life and soul out of me in the process. I doubted I would survive long enough to see whatever good the Bible claimed was on the other side of this endless nightmare. Christ showed me what led to my unwanted and unexplainable train wreck-level dis-

1

ruption, not just on every facet of my life but the lives of my husband, my kids, my entire family, and my social circles.

Christ took me through my childhood so I could see the roots of never wanting to feel out of control, how it shaped and impacted my decision-making into my adulthood. I learned why self-discipline and self-reliance failed under severe duress. More importantly, he showed me his divine fingerprints all over my life. How he needed to dump out all I thought I knew so he could fill me up with himself and his power to prepare me for confronting something no one else could fix.

Christ wanted me to understand I treated my illness like an obstacle or challenge I failed to overcome instead of as an invitation to trust him for a greater level of faith to leap that chasm. Could I really have the kind of faith that laughed in the face of utter hopelessness because I knew Christ could truly accomplish the impossible? I thought I knew the answer to that question until confronted with the brutal reality. What if this horrific pain lasted until the day I died? Buckle up, take this journey with me, and learn to see beyond your storm.

Once there were three children that were all moved to a one-hundred-year-old home in Nimy, Belgium, which had a secret room and a magical attic. Sounds like the opening of *The Lion, the Witch and the Wardrobe* by C. S. Lewis. I lived in Belgium during my second, third, and fourth-grade years, and my mom read us that wonderful book in that grand old house. We lived next door to our landlord known only as monsieur, who lived on a farm with puppies, rabbits, chickens, a pony, and a donkey.

My childhood memories are strange to me because so many are categorized by where we lived or the people we knew, more than anything else. My dad was enlisted in the US Air Force, and my mother stayed home with me and my brothers Ron (two years older than me) and Bryon (five years younger than me). My memories were dictated by locations because we moved, on average, about every year and a half throughout my childhood.

Ah, the life of a military brat. I have met many fellow armed services brats over the years and not all cherished the travel and dis-

Journey DERAILED

Is Your Hope for Healing Tied to a Diagnosis,
an Expected Outcome, a Cure, or to Christ?

RHONDA CASTANON

ISBN 979-8-88751-159-7 (paperback)
ISBN 979-8-88751-160-3 (digital)

Christian Faith Publishing
832 Park Avenue
Meadville, PA 16335
www.christianfaithpublishing.com

Printed in the United States of America

All journeys have secret destinations of
which the traveler is unaware.

—Martin Buber

ruption, but I loved it. That is, until our final family move, which sent me to a new state and a new school for my junior and senior years of high school. I was most unhappy about that last relocation

To this day, my most numerous and earliest vivid recollections are from when we lived in Europe. I did not have any actual concept of what a rare opportunity it was to live there. At the time, it was simply the next place I moved with my family. Europe was forever imprinted on my brain because of how many experiences that made me feel like I was living out my books. I was an avid reader who relished the adventures of *The Great Mouse Detective*, the *Narnia* series, *A Bear Called Paddington*, the *Hardy Boys* series, the *Nancy Drew* series, *The Bobbsey Twins* series, *Black Beauty*, *The Black Stallion*, *Man O' War*, *The White Pony* and *Brighty of the Grand Canyon* to name a few.

I loved visiting the castles that I read about in school. I went to Waterloo when I learned about Napoleon. I saw the Loch Ness Monster, Nessie, I swear. I pretended I was Sherlock Holmes as I wandered through stone-laid roads and watched the fog descend in Scotland. Yes, I know Holmes is British, but Scotland embodied the mood and imagery of so many of his adventures to me. I read about the Von Trapp Family, Anne Frank and secret rooms, and then I found one in our European home. My imagination was lit on fire all the time. Robin Hood was my hero, and I saw his tree in Sherwood Forest.

I can still picture the little neighborhood boy who lived across the street and the only word of French I understood: *jouer* (sounds like zhoou way), which meant "play." Our home included the coolest, best, full room-sized attic where Narnia came to life for me. The open market at the top of the alley we lived on was where we were always given free candy out of the crates of sweet delectables on display.

Our crazy singing babysitter—she literally sang sentences to us to pick up toys or clean the dishes instead of simply stating it to us in a normal tone of voice. I remember the missionaries we met and a Christian tent revival in England. I fell in love with Holland, the windmills, and getting my own pair of handmade clogs—you know, the ones you see in all the pictures of children from Holland. Did you know that they were actually comfortable? I used the clogs at Christmas so St. Nicholas could fill them with candy, and he did.

My scariest memory from Europe was a terrible public bus accident I was in with my mother, my youngest brother, and a family friend. We were the only people left on this large city bus as we traveled to my first gymnastics meet. It had just started to rain when the driver of a semitrailer truck lost control, skidded across the center median of the road into our opposite-facing traffic lane, and hit us nearly head on.

I saw the tractor trailer coming at us, and then it went black. Waking up in the bus, I saw the bloodied bus driver and the windshield all shattered. The bus was surrounded by people. I watched my mom check on the bus driver. I witnessed her desperately trying to pry and push open the bus door from the inside while others pulled from the outside.

I did not remember blacking out again, only waking up. I realized, someone took me out of the bus and placed me inside someone's car. I was all by myself. A sea of strange faces surrounded the car with countless eyes staring at me. Someone pounded on the car window. People spoke to me in French and gestured at me.

I tried to ask someone where my family was, but no one understood or seemed to be listening. It was so chaotic. I was placed in an ambulance by myself, along with the bus driver. The bus driver's anguished moans and groans terrified me. The ambulance beds were stacked like bunk beds, and I was on the top bunk but was not strapped in.

As the ambulance careened through the streets, I rolled helplessly side to side. *I'm going to slide right off this bed. I'm going to land right on top of the guy helping the bus driver.* I couldn't move my arms properly because I had broken my left collarbone and couldn't keep my grip on to the bed railings to help stabilize myself.

At the hospital, I don't recall anyone asking me anything; I was simply placed into a room. I'm still absolutely clueless where my parents were during any of this time. Remember, I was only in second grade. I lay in this room and genuinely believed I might never see my family again. The door to the adjoining room was left open. I watched, horrified as the slashed and bloodied bus driver was wheeled into that room. I saw his distraught wife and heard her hysterical wailing.

A short time later, a strange family came into my room, shook their heads, and said, "No, that's not my daughter." I was terrified! *Where's my family?* My mom and dad finally found me. Upon seeing my parents, I disintegrated into sobs as near-indescribable relief flooded through my body. I was transferred to an American ambulance where I was placed on the gurney, wrapped in blankets like a cocoon, and snugly strapped in. Someone spoke to me the whole time I was in the ambulance. I felt so warm and safe finally.

What a wild experience to endure as a child. What I couldn't fathom at the time was what a truly profound impact this accident had on the remainder of my life. This bus wreck was the springboard for a lifetime dance with control and self-reliance—actually, with not wanting to feel out of control of anything ever again. These were connections the Lord helped me make recently. The safety I felt in being goal oriented and driven grew deeper roots as I matured in age.

After Europe, we lived in Oklahoma during my fifth-grade year. Our family had it tougher in Oklahoma than I was certainly aware of as a child. I was utterly mesmerized by horses, which surrounded us, so all was well in my childish eyes. We lived in private housing, as opposed to on the military base, and money was tight. You know how we, as kids, say, "There's nothing to eat in this house." What we usually mean is, "I don't *see* anything I *want* to eat."

My older brother, Ron, upon finding the cabinets once again empty, asked our dad, "Does this mean we're poor?" In my dad's words, "Oklahoma was like no other time in our life. We struggled and skimped and scraped wherever we could. But alas, cupboards were often bare. Of course, there was spinach or wheat pasta varieties, carob (for those that don't know, carob is no-fun chocolate), and wannabe Cheerios and Rice Krispies. Times were definitely tough that year."

I still shiver thinking about the wheat and spinach pasta. Now I eat spinach pasta by choice. Back then though, that wheat pasta was stiff, pasty, and just plain gross tasting. After we left Oklahoma, we moved straight to our "home" away from home: Muir, Pennsylvania.

I coined Muir "the land time forgot" in nostalgic love for the pint-sized township, which contained the one constant "home" in my life: Nana and Papa's house (my mother's parents). Throughout my entire life, whenever I returned, the homes, the families, and the surroundings never changed. Both of my parents were from Pennsylvania as were both sets of grandparents.

My father had actually left the military and was now just a private citizen. Because of this major transition in my dad's livelihood plus the aftermath of Oklahoma, we did not have a place to live, and we did not have a lot of money. So we moved in with Nana and Papa.

Muir is a small, once-thriving, coal mining, and later, manufacturing township nestled in a valley surrounded by hills and mountains. It had one-stop sign and zero stoplights. Muir is the kind of wondrous place where everybody knew your name, at least your family name, and definitely knew the reputation of said family.

Luckily, my mother was a "darling" in school; everybody loved her. My dad had a more "bad boy" type of reputation. I walked down the street, and someone remarked, "You must be Sandy's [my mother] daughter"—pretty creepy when you're a kid. My high school was filled with teachers who also taught my parents those same classes when they were in high school. No lie, I had a history teacher who was a literal piece of living history, having been born in the late 1800s. Older than dirt, right?

We lived with Nana and Papa for approximately six months until we got our own home just a street over from them. I could literally walk out the back door of Nana and Papa's house, cross their backyard, the back alley, down the hill through one of my closest friends' yard, meander a few houses up the street to arrive at our new home. Our family attended the local Evangelical Church directly across from our home.

My dad attended seminary school and worked at our local post office, which, I swear to you, was like out of *The Andy Griffith Show*. It was one small building with a counter and a bunch of cubby hole slots for the mail to be inserted into. You didn't even need to use a full street address when you mailed something. I used to mail things to my grandparent's as "Nana and Papa Jones," the street name with no numerical needed, city, state, and zip code.

Even for phone calls, you only used the last digit of the first three numbers, along with the remaining four digits, to be connected to the other person. This was a major adjustment time for our family. My mom began working outside the home as a secretary in my high school, which taught grades 6 to 12 in one building.

All my dad, or the rest of the family, had ever known was military life and moving. Although there was a certain comfort because of living in Pennsylvania, our family continued to struggle. My parents got only the groceries we needed for meals, while luxuries, like soda or snack food, were a rare treat. As a child, I never knew my parents had a total of five jobs between them, trying to make ends meet.

Something else I never knew at the time: Those decisions were made to get our family off food stamps. Our financial struggles were the reason behind why we also started a vegetable garden and why my mother canned vegetables for us. For the *first* time, at the age of twelve, I had more awareness of what we had versus other families.

All my clothing for school were hand-me-downs from my aunt, my dad's half sister who was fourteen years younger than him. This was at the beginning of the eighties era. Teens only wore jeans and T-shirts in this remote area, except for two girls. Me, I owned one pair of jeans, but my other clothes were the stunning seventies decor of colored polyester pants and sweater vests. I was not exactly a fashionista.

Instead, I tried wearing my one and only pair of jeans every single day of school, much to my mother's horror and consternation. I'm in sixth grade with all the sweeping anxieties that go along with it. My friendship triangle consisted of my two closest school friends, and we were commonly split into factions whenever one got mad, leaving the third to choose sides.

The neighborhood gaggle of boys teased me mercilessly about my skinny legs and body. I dreaded leaving my house because I knew I would inevitably see them and have to listen to their harassment.

The town was too small; it was impossible to not run into them anytime I was outside more than half an hour.

In addition to all the normal early teen angst and anxiety over once again starting over, I had a life-altering experience with my hair. The only hairdresser in the area could have been a character out of the *Steel Magnolias* movie. The "salon" was in her home, and she coiffed every elderly lady's hair. Let me repeat, she did elderly ladies' hair. My mom sent me there when I wanted a wavy hair perm. I did not want to go there.

I saw how she did my Nana's hair, which looked great on her. But for me? My mom assured me I only had to explain what I wanted. How bad could it be, right? Well, it was the kind of almost permanently scarring experience that prevented me from ever wanting to step foot into another salon ever again.

Let me paint the picture before you think I'm exaggerating this experience. My friend and neighbor, Terri, went with me for moral support. Terri sat, waited, and watched. For my part, I did tell the hairdresser what I wanted: waves, wavy hair. I watched in abject horror as these miniscule, little rollers were placed all over my skull. I was uselessly repeating to myself not to panic; it would look different once she dried my hair. *Not!* My mortification was not yet complete.

As she removed the extra small rollers from my hair, all I could see was row upon row of tightly wound curlicues. Horrified by the sight of tiny caterpillar shaped tubes all over my head, I wanted to bolt, screaming from the chair. Instead, politeness and I think utter shock kept me rooted to my seat. I couldn't take my eyes off the mirror. I became Dorothy from *The Wizard of Oz*, repeating silently to myself, "There's no place like home. There's no place like home."

How I wished I could've teleported in that moment. I envisioned it, wished it to become a possibility. My mind was tripping all over itself, trying to picture which way I could run home in the hopes of never seeing a solitary soul. I could not even look at my friend. I did not want to see her face. I could not bear looking at my own reflection. When my transformation was complete, I looked like my Nana.

My hair was teased and as round and puffy as a cotton ball; I kid you not. My friend was so traumatized; she refused to walk home with me. In fact, she ran all the way home. *What is she running for, I'm the one wearing the beehive.* Her quick retreat further sank my already devastated heart into believing I would never, ever, ever be able to show my face to anyone again.

My stomach rolled and pinched in anguish over how I was going to get on the bus, let alone face anyone at school on Monday. I ended up being grateful my friend left me behind so I could cry my eyes out. My feet couldn't carry me quickly enough, nor could my head swivel fast enough. I desperately scanned every possible avenue by which I might be seen before busting through the safety of my home. I was near hysterical by the time I exploded through my front door. I think I was actually wailing the millisecond I crossed the threshold of my house.

My mother's assurances that it wasn't that bad fell on inconsolable ears. I was convinced my life, as I knew it, was over. When I went to school on Monday, my own homeroom teacher thought I was a *brand-new* student coming into class for the first time. She even said the words while she walked toward me before she caught herself, realizing a little too late that it was me.

The whole class turned to look at this supposed new student, only to see me standing there like a deer caught in headlights—ugh, the devastation, humiliation, and embarrassment I felt. I learned something though. I discovered, emotions could be controlled. If you put on a game face and met the ridicule head on, even when it felt as if the jeering lasted a lifetime, people eventually moved on, and the norm returned.

Oddly enough, I think that "Nightmare on Hair Street" underpinned what became my conviction about dating, guys, and my body. What was the connection between the perm debacle and those convictions? I think it went back to understanding what I felt in the moment did not necessarily dictate the end result, let alone the forever result. I could get through anything and still be okay.

I discovered my conviction about dating guys, in my seventh-grade year, when a new boy joined our grade. Our school rarely added new students. Sheesh, was he the hot topic of discussion among practically every girl in the school. He was tall and good-looking, and he was fresh meat. He was clueless to the competition he sparked among the local girls. My girlfriend's "look at me" race was on.

I saw no need to join the clamor for his attention. I did not think I was ugly, but I did not see myself as the kind of girl that guys would be fighting each other to ask out compared to my girlfriends. I found this competitiveness over guys silly. I watched my girlfriends bounding around the new guy, trying to outperform each other to beguile him, dressing to attract him, pretending to be interested in the same things, and pretending to be dumber than they really were, all to get and to keep his attention. *How could you want a guy to like you under false pretenses?* It seemed senseless to me to argue with another girl or drop a friendship over a guy. If the guy chose another girl over you, what are you mad at her for? Why would you still want to pursue him after that? It was inexplicable to me.

I made a landmark decision that year that stayed with me the rest of my life. The decision was, if a guy couldn't like me for exactly who I was and what I looked like, then he wasn't worth my time. I certainly wasn't going to change my personality or interests to get his attention. For what purpose? The real kicker? The new guy singled me out.

He specifically arranged to meet me in our gym, which was filled with gymnastics equipment. I interpreted his flirtatiousness as not real and just to see if he could get me to fawn all over him too. We laughed and talked while he showed off on the gymnastic rings hanging from the ceiling rafters. To my surprise, he saw right through most of my friend's admiration acts and claimed it was why he was not dating any of them.

I never bragged to my friends about that time. I kept it my secret. I told myself he was just being nice. I was safe to talk with because I never threw myself at him. Inwardly, I knew I was more concerned my classmates would tease me about liking him. Even more, I feared *he* would ridicule me if people even thought I was implying he was interested in me because I dared to tell anyone about our gym time together. I kept my mouth shut.

Oddly enough, this one pivotal interaction created opposing reactions within me that spilled into my overall future outlook and life. I internalized a deepened sense of empowerment over what I perceived as emotional control and decision-making capabilities but was only a mask for a false sense of security in myself. On one hand, with female friendships, I was always concerned about what if I lose her as a friend or disappointed her. But with guys, I adopted a cavalier attitude of "don't let the door hit ya where the good Lord split ya."

Ultimately, trying to keep those masks in place spiraled into a surreptitious deadening of my overall emotions in order to ensure no one knew how they really made me feel. I controlled my facial expressiveness and my outward display of emotions. Some of the unforeseen fallout of that "power"? I sought female friendships but never dating relationships. I chose girlfriends but stumbled into guy relationships.

I use "chose" loosely because, in all reality, almost all of my relationship choices were based mostly on instinct and connection as opposed to some substantive commonality between us. What ran underneath this false power was control. I didn't know it then, but control just tightened its first monkey paw onto my back.

Besides my neighbor Terri, my two closest friends were Nat (short for Natalie) and LeeAnn. We were a tight trio. However, our threesome was often divided into various combinations of twosomes with one invariably feeling miffed toward another. Boy, did I learn problem-solving skills from our constant silly bickering, which always boiled down to minor misunderstandings. LeeAnn became my *first* unknowing encounter with Holy Spirit.

I had a dream. I clearly saw LeeAnn walk into our school cafeteria where we all gathered after the bus drop-off and before first period. She wore a long camel-colored coat with the hood up and her skirt peeking out from under the coat. She had long socks and her shoes on. She walked over to us. I knew Nat was with me, but I did not visually see her. LeeAnn smiled with her perfect and brilliantly white teeth glowing. She whipped back her hood and revealed a boy-short haircut. It was not a buzz cut, just cropped super short all over her head and did not go over her ears.

The dream unnerved me because of the colors and vivid detail. I saw her face, and it was her. I have had lots of dreams where I do not ever see faces or not clearly, or they look like someone else, but I knew it was "xyz" person. Heading off for school the following morning, I was giddy, knowing what a kick Nat and LeeAnn were going to get when I tell them about my dream. I saw Nat first. I excitedly told her I had the funniest dream about LeeAnn, but I did not want to give details until LeeAnn arrived.

With my little eye, I spied—camel. Dumbfounded, my stare traced LeeAnn's every step as she closed in on Nat and me. My dream had just stepped into living color. My eyes took in what she wore. *This cannot be.* I saw the exact coat, the hood hiding her head, the exact skirt, and the exact shoes. It was incredulous. Out of the corner of my vision, I saw Nat staring at me, staring at LeeAnn.

Holding my breath, I waited for LeeAnn to remove her hood. My brains fumbling over the fact she walked all the way into the school building, into the cafeteria, all the way down the walkway, and crossed over half the length of this room and never removed her hood. Standing in front of us, she triumphantly threw back her hood to show off her trendy new, short haircut. My mouth gaped open.

LeeAnn self-consciously fingered her coif and tentatively asked if it looked that bad. Still stunned, I blurted out, "I dreamed this. I dreamed you cut your hair." They both responded with blank-faced stares. Out of embarrassment and shock, I do not remember retelling the details of my dream to either of them. It was too juicy to not discuss at least a little, but I quickly shifted the conversation back to LeeAnn and what spurred her decision. You do not understand what a big deal this was at our school.

Virtually, no one broke the mold or wore anything expensive other than name-brand jeans or ever tried to *style* their hair according to the latest trends. Kids in this small town got haircuts not makeovers. A strange sensation stayed with me the entire day and for a number of days afterward. Part of the unease I felt was because the dream showed me the ridicule she'd receive and how we needed to come around her as her friends.

So I knew to do that, to specifically tell her to ignore people's comments, how much guts it took to do, and how beautiful she looked. Unfortunately, I did not see this as a work of the Holy Spirit. I buried the memory instead. I had never said anything to anyone about this dream until about two years ago. I never even thought to ask my parents about the dream. It seemed weird, and so I ignored it.

After two and a half years in Pennsylvania, my father rejoined the military, and we moved to Florida in time for the second half of my eighth-grade year. Immediately, I fell in love with Florida. I mean, what's not to love about sunshine, sand, and the sea? Moving to Florida played a decisive role in my teen life, my outlook on religion/faith but also in my future.

In eighth grade, I had an abysmal experience at a private Southern Baptist school. I quickly discovered two extremes within the student body, the strictly religious versus the delightfully determined delinquent. My recently discovered emotional control served me well against my first female-threatened beat down. What happened to me? Valerie happened. Valerie was the classic bad girl who seemed to relish her reputation.

I will just tell you, before you begin to wonder what smart-alecky kind of thing I did to deserve being cornered, outnumbered, and outflanked; I did absolutely nothing. I mean it. I was the new girl. Valerie was warning me to not even *think* about looking at her man. I had never spoken to her boyfriend, but that minor fact did not matter either. I was cornered in a small conference room space within the main classroom area. Do not ask me where the teacher was or went, I have no recollection of any of that.

I faced Valerie and her fleet of willing, and not so willing, compatriots. Everyone was afraid of Valerie. In fact, I was warned about her, and her boyfriend was pointed out to me so that I'd know who to avoid glancing at every day. Why did she close ranks on me? She was just ensuring I received the message from her directly. Rather kind of her, don't you think? Control kicked in.

I knew Valerie's reputation. I knew I was all alone; I was surrounded, and I did not want to die. Somehow, all those thoughts converged inside my brain and willed my legs to support me, ani-

13

mated my mouth, and allowed me to remain emotionally calm, cool, and collected. Valerie closed ranks on me with fists and teeth tightly clenched. She was intentionally backing me into the farthest corner of the conference room so I could not be seen if the teacher reentered the main classroom.

The semicircle of antagonists was partly to shield and partly to stand guard. Valerie was so hostile, like bottled-up rage. I do not know a better description of her demeanor. She did not have any specific accusation, just general threats of what her boyfriend allegedly said, rumors she heard, and simply just making sure I did not get any idiotic ideas to muscle in on her turf. I decided to stand my ground, not retreat any further, listened to each insult she hurled at me, and calmly responded to her.

At some point, it seemed as if all the pent-up energy eventually dissipated. Valerie made her final threat for me to stay clear of her boyfriend, turned heels, and left with her gaggle of female followers, trailing behind her out of that room. I audibly exhaled as soon as she was gone. I breathed deep, gathered myself, and returned to the classroom.

I survived Hurricane Valerie, untouched and unharmed. No kidding. My encounter with Valerie was the hot topic at school the next day. To say I dreaded going to school after that would be an understatement of the largest proportions. Desperately, I tried to keep a low profile and avoided both Valerie and her boyfriend. However, the following week, I had my next encounter with Valerie at the outdoor basketball court.

It was peaceful on the court, beautiful weather that day. I was all alone, just passing the time until I was picked up. Then I heard someone call out to me. Ugh, I knew that voice. I turned. My heart sank. It was Valerie. Rumors had buzzed all over school that sooner or later she'd get me. No one survived Valerie. So I thought, *This is it. She'll beat me into a pulp, and there isn't a soul around to save me.* Instead, a most remarkable thing occurred; she apologized for her behavior.

She didn't say "I'm sorry" directly, but she was definitely baffled by my behavior. I didn't tell on her. I did not bad-mouth her with fellow students. I did not fight back when she had me cornered. My behavior truly confounded her, and she wanted to know why. So I told her. I had no issue with her. I had zero interest or intent toward her boyfriend. I saw no point in dancing fisticuffs with her. We played basketball as we talked, and she opened up to me.

Valerie divulged things to me about her attitude, her family, and even about her boyfriend. I told her I thought her boyfriend kind of liked getting her riled up and watching her fight over him based on something I saw him do once in the school hallway. She knew what I was talking about and agreed with me. Truly, what was even more astonishing than not getting knocked out by Valerie was becoming friends. This incident became another feather in my proverbial emotional-control cap.

I didn't see that miracle as Christ protecting me or as a blessing stemming from what the Bible means by a kind word turning away wrath or being kind to your enemy is like heaping burning coals upon their head. Instead, I saw proof that controlling your emotions works.

This encounter on the court with her also demonstrated that bully behavior can be a cover-up for deep, personal pain, trauma, and insecurity—a lesson that would serve me well in my next couple of high schools, in my college interests, my early career, as a lawyer, and as a mom.

For my freshman year in high school, it was once again my joy to be a new student at another Chrisitan school, regular Baptist this time, which was a much better experience for both my brother, Ron, and I. Plus, the spiritual soul versus bad boy/girl dynamic was present but not as extreme. I had many firsts at this school: my first "serious" dating relationship with a senior, French-kissing, wearing a bikini, and staring down shyness.

Laurel represented everything I wanted to be. She was outgoing, fun, loved to laugh, goofy, kind, generous, confident but unpretentious, and the trendiest dresser I'd ever met. She defied every Christian kid stereotype embedded in my head. She was the reason I learned to beat my bashfulness. She was a junior like my brother, Ron, and we hit it off. It was hard not to like her. She had such an infectious laugh. She never once made me feel like she just tolerated me.

Laurel had a knack for sweeping you up in her whirlwind of joy and peppiness. She challenged my thinking about why I was timid. I think she literally looked at it that way. Why? Why be shy? For what purpose? What was I afraid would happen? Well, I had no answers for her. Why didn't I wear a bikini? Well, I was too skinny. She said I had the kind of body that people expected to see in a bikini. What was wrong with being skinny? So I lamented how I was terribly teased for being so stick straight. Her response? Pish posh, stupid boys. Ignore them.

She handed me a bikini, told me to put it on. And when she saw me, she said, "See, you look great!" So simple but life transforming, not because of the bikini but her matter-of-factness about the whole thing. It was as if she pulled off the veil and showed me myself for the first time. She unknowingly confirmed for me how emotions can be manipulated. It took one person. One.

One person who simply mentioned, in the course of ordinary conversation, a positive to being thin—and it was like a light bulb going off for me. Why did I let what other people thought or said determine what I should believe, especially about myself? Another point scored in empowerment's corner. Again, I learned emotions were a very fickle thing; they can lie to you. Emotions can be switched on or off and back and forth between positive and negative.

Crawling out of my turtle shell of shyness, I metamorphosed into tenth grade with a whole new emotional outlook, which was at, yet, another school: Satellite High in Satellite Beach, Florida. Go Scorpions! I loved that school. *I am Rhonda. Hear me roar.* Don't get me wrong, I still felt the normal "shark bait" type of anxiety from swimming into unknown and foreign school waters, but I challenged myself to dive right in.

I wanted this year to be different. The same public school that didn't pan out so well for my brother, Ron, changed my life in so many ways, both good and bad. I *so* wanted to be a Scorpionette. The Scorpionettes were some of the prettiest girls in the school, it seemed, and they were the dance squad for the football team. Honestly, the real draw just might have been the outfits—so sparkly and sassy.

Here I was, going from wishing I was a flower on a wall to considering whether or not I was brave enough to try out for the Scorpionettes. Talk about a 180-degree turnabout. I did not try out for that squad. I guess, the mental switch felt safer staying inside my head instead of showing itself in my outward behavior. The scrawny kid I thought I mentally buried was still alive and well after all.

Satellite High was a radically different school experience. It was the first time everything just clicked into place for me. From making such a wide variety of friends to the inclusiveness of the student body, female friends who didn't play down their intelligence and who had college goals, testing my flirting mettle with guys, the party dynamic and being able to drive all converged together to make for a wild school year.

We had our factions like all high schools—surfers, skaters, stoners, jocks, and military brats, to name a few—but everyone seemed to hang out and party together outside of school. One of my favorite memories, to this day, was how the sea of salt-spray bleached white hair of the surfer crowd always miraculously disappeared from the school library whenever the surf was good. The surfers sat in one section of the library so all you would see was row after row of mostly white, blond hair—no whitewash of hair when the waves were worthy.

Was it all just a matter of perception? What was so uniquely different about Satellite High? In part, I knew it was my attitude and the many "firsts" mentioned above, all occurring within that one year. Sometimes it seemed more like the end of an innocence era for me—innocence as to the time, not what I did. A lot of "firsts" were broken in tenth grade, such as being chased by the police and visiting the police station, drinking and partying, flirting, dirty dancing, and finally kissing the one guy who set my heart aflutter all year.

Interestingly enough, I also encountered the beginnings of discerning the still, small voice inside me. I failed to recognize this voice as Holy Spirit, but I ascertained its value. One such example was the prompting that a party was spiraling out of control, and I needed to leave right away. The party thrower's rule was simple: Everyone was to remain inside the house, no loitering outside. Well, as the word spread about the party and the number of people ballooned, so did the mass of partygoers wandering around out front of the house.

All I recalled was this warning bell going off inside my head; things were turning ugly. Way too many people outside, and I knew the cops were going to be called sooner rather than later. Luckily, I listened to that unease and left. A resounding bonne chance, not just because my inklings turned out to be correct. The cops were called.

Even worse, to my teenage mind, somehow my parents got wind of the party. I don't recall if it was because my brother was supposed to pick me up and couldn't find me or what. I'll never forget the scene when I arrived home. My dad and brother were sitting in the living room, facing the door, clearly waiting for me. I threw open the door and the look on my brother's face, as my brain catches up to my eyes, sent an instantaneous message: Do not…say…a…word.

The running joke in my family was, you always knew when dad was really, truly upset if his ears were bright red, but his mouth was not moving. His ears were glowing like Rudolph's nose—oh so bright. Well, my father drove to that party and saw teens passed out on the front lawn and other such delightful things, looking for me. Fortunately, I had already vacated the premises.

Actually, my dad even said words to that effect, "It's a good thing I didn't find you there." Sounded like we had literally just missed one another. I breathed such a sigh of relief that I listened to that clanging bell inside my brain. It was a lesson that locked in place for me: heed those warnings.

However, one of the times I failed to respond to that inner voice had high ramifications, which could've forever marred my future. Excited barely covered how I felt the very first time I went out with my soon-to-be closest friend, Nikki. She drove me to someone's townhouse because she knew a certain boy, I thought was so adorable, would be there. We did not know the guy who owned the apartment, but we learned he was a recent fellow alma mater graduate. We did not know his reputation with the cops.

At some point, we came out of the apartment and started talking with our host, Martin, who sat on the ground, leaning against the pillar outside his front doorway, and smoked a cigarette. The cops pulled up, got out, and started chatting Martin up. They said quite derogatory things about him, the kind that send your stomach to your toes. The cops simply harassed him because he was outside. They knew him, and they could.

Their primary concern seemed to be if we knew who he was. I wanted to leave, but I didn't drive. We answered the police officers' questions. They joyously filled us in on his police reputation—not good, not terrible, just stupid stuff, but it still made my heart race. We went inside, and the cops left after a bit. Nikki and I went back inside, walked upstairs, when we heard a loud thud, voices, then a couple of our guy friends flew up the stairs and yelled, "Cops! Run!"

My brain went blank and, like automatons, Nikki and I both followed the flow of teens and leaped off the second-floor balcony. We ran at breakneck speed. Everyone scattered in all directions, and you could hear the cops yelling from behind us. I had no clue where I was going; I just followed Nikki. We raced to the local 7-Eleven where I promptly grabbed the pay phone to call my parents.

Well, wouldn't you know, the cops pulled up right behind us, the same two officers who spoke with us outside the apartment. I was dumbfounded at how they knew where we would end up…and so quickly. Of course it was logical. The police officers knew we were on foot, so naturally, we would need a ride; hence the need for a pay phone.

Yes, pay phone. These were the days before pocket cell phones. The cops provided us with the delight of calling our parents from the police station. We were never arrested or even officially detained. Between our earlier responses to their inquiries as to our connections to Martin and the fact I was caught in the process of dialing my parents at the 7-Eleven boded well for us.

Talk about a most uncomfortable conversation to have with your parents. I never, in a million years, would've even conceived I'd be in such a jam. How quickly life can spiral out of control. How lightning, seemingly fast innocent circumstances, can change in a flip of a coin. I warned myself to stay more vigilant in the future.

Christ spared me from being arrested. I never recognized his grace. We had been drinking beer, and we were clearly underage. Christ was honing my hearing—fine, tuning my Holy Spirit GPS. Christ was teaching me how to hear him, how to develop convictions, and learning how to respond immediately. I thought I was just a quick study.

Most of our high school parties and gatherings didn't take place inside residences. We had a local, unused racetrack where half the school lined up and parked to drink and carouse during most weekends. People didn't seem to fight or feel a need to be destructive or stupid. Everyone just hung out. It was a gathering spot where you drove or walked up and down the strip, chatted, and drank alcohol.

No one ever made me feel pressured to drink. It was there, someone might ask, but if I said, "No," no one seemed to care. I did experiment with drinking and discovered the good, the bad, and the ugly about this activity. The bad, I learned what blacking out meant. The good thing is, I learned what blacking out meant. The ugly, realizing what could have happened during my first blackout.

For this particular episode, we were convened in an unfinished subdivision. A couple of my guy friends noticed one particular guy, the cute but quiet one who rarely showed up at the party scene, leading me away from the crowds toward one of the partially built homes. He had his arm around my neck and pulled me close to him. My guy friends leaped into rescue mode and returned me to safety. All I could recall was him whispering to me and keeping me close.

I had no other awareness of what was occurring. I did not remember talking or being led away. I had hazy recollections of sitting in a friend's car and hearing them speak about me and to me, as if they were disembodied voices in my head. The next day, I heard all the gritty details. Mortification filled me. It was unfathomable that the "quiet" guy had ill-intent in isolating me, but what else could he have been up to?

Naively, since no one in my family drank, and I rarely even remember a wine bottle in any of our homes, I thought blacking out from alcohol consumption was something that happened only to established alcoholics, not novices. What was "good" about blacking out? Well, it deeply rooted in a conviction that I never, ever wanted to feel out of control or unaware of my surroundings again. What could have happened that night terrified me.

Parties also showed me drunk people kind of suck. I didn't want to be "that" person. Amazing how one episode epitomized how dramatically different people can be when intoxicated, how the persona a guy displayed in public was not always the same in private. Valuable lessons indeed. Making sure I stayed wary of my surroundings and disciplined about my own behavior was further reinforced by two other demoralizing incidents.

The next blow to my sense of personal security was, one night, my brother, Ron, and I were together somewhere with some mutual friends. A friend of one of his friends drove me home from wherever we were. My inner voice whispered caution when he offered, but I dismissed it as being ridiculous. This guy was well regarded, and he had been very polite and well-behaved the entire evening. However, that all changed on the way home. He chatted with me during the drive.

He constantly chided me for sitting at the extreme opposite end of the bench seat in his car. Finally, I relented and moved slightly closer. He stopped prior to the bridge that led to the beachside homes and military housing where I lived. He wanted to kiss me. I felt sick and angry I was in this position but convinced myself it was harmless or how else was I going to get home now? I stuffed my fear down inside so I could try to think what to do.

Kissing was not enough. I froze. My mind swirled with colliding thoughts of panic. *Can I run? I can't do this. I can't speak.* He began coaxing me into a sexual act against my will. I was still a virgin; I had never done anything like this before. I just wanted it to be over. I wanted him to take me home. I had no way to call someone and would have a really long walk home if he kicked me out of the car or hit me. I had no clue what to expect from him anymore.

Once it was all over, he drove me home and dropped me off with a wave and a smile. It only dawned on me later how calculated

21

and strategized he had been about the whole thing. It took me weeks to gather the nerve to tell Ron what happened. He exploded. I think he was madder at himself because it happened at all. He was supposed to drive me home.

I was relieved at his anger because it wasn't directed at me. I felt so ashamed. I never let him say a word to anyone, nor did I, for years. I buried the whole thing as deep into the far recesses of my mind as I could manage. I compartmentalized my emotions. People are not always what they seem. How I see or what I feel about something or someone does not equate to how someone else sees me or that same situation.

A mandatory move? The words shattered and ricocheted through my mind. *How can the military make you move? How is that possible?* I imploringly pleaded with my dad. I was in poorly restrained agony as I posed this question because of the sheer effort required to maintain my composure and to *not* yell at my dad. My blissful dream of an awesome high school experience, to start college in Florida and to live forever in Florida instantaneously, dissolved. As I jested earlier, *Oh, the joys of military life.*

Instead of retiring in Florida as expected and planned, my dad was needed for one final move, this time to Colorado. No options. Do not pass. *Go.* Do not collect $200. I should've been ecstatic at the opportunity to see such a beautiful state as Colorado, but all I could see was what I was losing. I would be losing great friends, a great school, an awesome beach, and amazing weather.

I had to start all over yet again. My brother, Ron, refused to go to Colorado with us. He was eighteen, don't you know? He was in love, like marry kind of love, don't you know? I had no idea what was happening to my family. Ron, in fact, stayed behind and lived with his girlfriend's family. He did not even have a full-time job when he made this brilliant, thoroughly reasoned decision. *No.* We left Florida at the end of my sophomore year.

All packed up and regretting to go, with our clothes, food, family, and our dog, all "giddily" sandwiched into a Pontiac Sunbird and a 1985 280Z, we began the 1,800-mile trek to Colorado Springs, Colorado, from Florida. Along the way, we had our own movie version of *Vacation*-style family histrionics. Memories like watching my father, in blinding rain, leaning with his head out of his window, holding a makeshift windshield wiper, slopping at the deluge of water dumping onto his windshield because the wipers weren't working.

I was sorely in need of an attitude adjustment when my junior year kicked off at Rampart High, Colorado Springs, Colorado. The school was brand-new, and I would be part of its first graduating class 1987. Contending with a "serious" boyfriend, dealing with a Debbie Downer-type closest friend, and nursing a wounded pride dominated that year. *I absolutely do not want to be here,* the statement emphatically resounded inside my head. My eyes assessed my latest high school, which really was impressive. It was a fully enclosed brick building with vaulted ceilings and gigantic glass windows overlooking the mountains, compared to Satellite High's 1970's multiple, single-story buildings stretched in grid-like patterns, college-campus style.

Unlike the brick-and-mortar surroundings, the students did not make a similarly jaw-dropping impression on me. People were closed, standoffish, and protective of their cliques, which I was continuously told was due to the considerable number of military students who were there one day or year then gone the next day, month, or year.

I hated hearing that. I had just left a Florida military base and a high school filled with military brats and most tended to be *friendly* precisely because we were in the military. At the time, I failed to see how *my own* less-than-sparkling outlook and attitude might have turned off or turned people away *from me,* too blinded by my own self-centeredness to comprehend that my mistake was looking outside myself, to people, and circumstances instead of internally at Christ, for my sense of stability, contentment, and need for belonging.

Near dread filled me every school day early in my junior year, primarily for many of the normal reasons, such as, would I have someone to sit with at lunch today? Would I start to meet more people or feel more connected ever at all to anyone or anything? Added to that angst was the inexplicable hatred aimed at me within the first weeks of school. Sitting in the cafeteria, this girl approached me.

She pointed my attention to this punk rock—adorned, white-blond, bi-level-haired girl scowling at me two or three tables away, who was sitting in my direct line of sight. I was informed, Ms. Punk Rock really hated me. I turned back to my informer, who I did not know either, and said, "Okay (awkward pause), she was entitled to feel that way, but I was new here, and I had never seen her before. I did not know who she was."

My informer stood stock-still in front of me. Apparently, I gave her a most unexpected response because she added, "But she really hates you. Watch out. She will be looking for you." I simply repeated, I did not know her, and I had no beef with her. Gee, what a grand welcome. Nothing ever came of the threat. In fact, I never did meet Ms. Punk Rock, nor did I ever find out why she hated me.

Eventually, I saw her again, but each time, I got a nod of acknowledgment or even a small smile. Oh, the fun of high school. This small incident brought further credence to the power of controlling my emotions. The Bible never entered the picture for me. I was saved, but I had no relationship with Christ or his Word. Once again, I didn't recognize the truth of God's Word that "a gentle answer turns away wrath" (Proverbs 15:1). In reality, my emotions were only being suppressed. A mindset of "never let them see you sweat" permanently locked itself into my life.

What? I can graduate at the end of my junior year? My guidance counselor informed me that, based on the number of credits I'd already accumulated, I could graduate. This was my chance to return to Florida sooner, to start college sooner, and to be out of *this* school sooner. Naturally, I said, "No." *Teen* logic, I can hear you snicker at that phrase precisely because it's instantly recognized as the oxymoron that it is while simultaneously encapsulating the life of a teenager.

You think you are smart. You feel smart. Grades may "prove" you contain intelligence. However, teens are not smart. Teen gray matter still needs training wheels. We use our adolescent brains like some maturity-o-meter self-assessment tool, convincing ourselves that we can unerringly gauge what a "mature" decision is in every and any situation. *Silly bear, teens really can't handle anything.*

For as desperately as I wanted to permanently shuttle off to Florida, there were choices to make first—decisions like, did I want to walk the stage and receive my diploma? Did I really want to start college at sixteen? If I did, how would I be treated? Would I later regret missing senior prom and the senior trip, the traditional graduation ceremony, and its surrounding pomp and circumstance?

My family would be missing all of those landmarks as well. Would I feel ready for a college lifestyle? Sorting through all these questions felt so monumental because I wanted some sort of assurance I was making the right decision. Oddly enough, the Holy Spirit did show me, but I had no spiritual eyes to notice. Whenever I thought of leaving, I felt this strange, unsettling tug in my heart, something just felt all wrong. When I thought of staying, my heart felt calm, and my "little voice" would say, "You know you need to just stay."

I struggled to accept this choice. If I'd been more Bible savvy, I would've recognized that "voice" as Christ rather than believing I was following my gut. In the end, I stopped the internal warfare raging inside my head; the peaceful feeling was too strong. I decided to stay in Colorado and graduate. Christ was speaking, but my ears were too plugged up with my own ideas about how to navigate my life.

Eventually, I made friends and enjoyed some of my classes and classmates, but I really only found a couple females, one of which lived near me, who I palled around with outside of school. I found myself spending most of my time with Alicia. She had such a sarcastically funny, almost acerbic, sense of humor, which I needed and wanted.

My psyche didn't connect that my necessity and desire for her constant carping was spawned out of how it temporarily helped soothe the heart of the roiling, discontent beast within me. However, later, as I met people and found new things to enjoy, I began to see her sarcasm as simply the thin veil for anger that it really was for both of us. What a painful awakening for me, which led to the end of that friendship—more unrecognized work of the Holy Spirit trying to garner my attention.

How do I now know it was the Holy Spirit? *He took an everyday experience and allowed me to see it with brand-new eyes, which ushered in undeniable conviction.* One of the Holy Spirit's favorite things to do is to make us more Christlike. Holding onto anger and resentment was not what the Lord wanted for me. To this day, I can envision sitting in her house, on a set of steps, as we just hung out and talked. Suddenly, it was like I heard her for the first time. I realized how often I had encouraged her lately to not be so down or sarcastic or trying to provide her with an alternative perspective to consider over some ordinary thing that happened to her.

It dawned on me, *I'm correcting her, but haven't I been doing and saying many of the same things?* The weight of that internal rebuke hung like a millstone around my neck. My body felt physically sick from that illumination. In that moment, I knew I had to change, and so did Alicia, or I could not keep hanging out with her so much. It was like being slapped.

How foolish I'd been to not see how much I needed to change or to grasp how churlish I'd become. The friendship didn't immediately end but seemed to fade into the distance as we steadily grew further apart. The Holy Spirit had some more revelations in store to mature me and my outlook.

One of the most surprising things I did was getting accepted into a brand-new peer counseling program the school started. The class was kept intentionally small, and we learned a lot of counseling and psychology-oriented material. We learned under what circumstances to involve the school guidance counselor or another administrator, and we practiced mock interviews and counseling sessions and a trust retreat.

There was one particular guy in my class who seemed determined to remain prickly toward me. He was never downright rude, but he made his dislike patently clear. His demeanor befuddled me until, one day, we had a direct confrontation right in the middle of class. I don't remember what we were discussing, but I used an example from my recent past, which happened in Florida, and that was the tipping point.

He retorted in disgust and said something along the lines of "If you love it so much in Florida, why don't you just go back there? It's all you talk about. I'm sick of hearing about it." His words deeply stung me. Honestly, I wasn't even sure how to respond to him at first. I was embarrassed since he blurted it out in front of everybody, but I also didn't feel I had said anything wrong or inappropriate.

When I did respond, I remembered apologizing and stating that the incident I mentioned happened in Florida. I did also acknowledge that I intended to return to Florida for college; it was where I lived before coming here, and I simply shared a relevant story. To my recollection, that confrontation allowed us further opportunity to flush out our feelings and allowed us to positively move forward. It also added another feather in my emotional control cap of how harnessing emotions really was a good thing, and I was good at it.

The final phase of this peer counseling course was to meet our first potential student client, which ended up being two females. They were either sisters or best friends who insisted on staying together. First, they met with each one of us, talked with us, and determined with whom they felt most confident and comfortable in order to move onto a private, one-on-one session. Stunningly, they both selected me, and they insisted on meeting with me together.

My teacher informed me that they both felt I made them feel safe and at ease. She wanted me to appreciate what a compliment this was and to feel proud of myself. Shock was my predominant emotional reaction to her words. Inwardly, a jumbled mix of fear, anxiety, pride, and elation churned in my belly and my brain. *Wow, would I be able to meet their expectations?*

Both the girls had some pretty heavy-duty issues we discussed. Man, what a humbling experience. We concluded by determining some specific next steps for them each to take and a follow-up if they were willing. This course and that counseling experience became a giant impetus for pulling me out of my emotional shell and improving my school year. *God was watering the seeds of an implanted desire to come alongside people and to help them.*

I had my first committed relationship in my junior year. His name was Tim, and we started dating right toward the beginning of the year. In hindsight, I fell into this relationship due, in part, to my unacknowledged loneliness. I purposely use the words "fell into" because I allowed it to happen more than I chose it. He made me laugh, took me places, and was a ton of fun. Why shouldn't I keep spending time with him?

We dated in those final years of high school where maybe, just maybe, he could be my soulmate, and we could get married after college. We dated the entire year, but I broke up with him early in our senior year. *The breakup was more about this unsettled feeling the relationship needed to end but for no specific reason I could see—another Holy Spirit prompting unknowingly ignored.*

I lost my virginity to Tim—losing, what an odd choice of words used in that commonly spoken phrase, as if I accidentally tripped and landed naked on my boyfriend. I gave a very precious part of myself away. There were several factors that contributed to this decision but one I did not comprehend—the impact of suppressed emotions.

Tim never made me feel pressured ever. He knew I was a virgin, and he took that quite seriously. His mother was almost borderline inappropriately open with him about sex. On one hand, I admired their openness and frankness with each other. On the other hand, she sometimes treated him like an adult best friend you tell everything.

She made sure I knew how open she was, that she preferred for him to have sex with her knowledge and stressed the practice of safe sex and to never push a girl ever. "No is no," she would say. We had free reign to have sex in his bedroom. I do not recall how long we dated before that monumental decision, but I do recall the boiling mix of thoughts spinning through my brain.

I kept it rational though. I ignored my emotions related to the decision. I loved Tim. I knew he would be fine waiting for me. It cannot be wrong if you are in love, right? Isn't this how it was supposed to be with someone you love? In the end, I drew a logical conclusion. I emphatically knew Tim deeply loved me, and I loved him. I felt safe, and I decided he would be the one.

Now do not get me wrong. It was not a robotic or quick decision, but I kept all the girly stuff out of the way. I had confidence in my and Tim's relationship. Our sexual desire was born out of love, not simple teenage lust to get laid or because it was expected; so I told myself. That was what I meant by keeping it rational. I compartmentalized my other emotions of guilt or disappointment (mine as well as my parents') or what preachers said, "Into a mental box," because emotions were fickle and could not be trusted.

Logic can be trusted, right? *How deeply I lied to myself by mistaking rationalization for logic.* I fell into the same trap so many others do, who lack any proper understanding of what the Bible actually says about sex and why it was designed for marriage. I heard premarital sex was bad, but I had no context for why. Why wasn't I taught the beautiful unity and bond this private act was meant to foster between the couple?

I never understood God's design for sex. I only knew sex sure was portrayed as the most amazing thing ever. The result, I did not dare look to the Bible, instead I did what seemed "natural" so it could not be truly "bad," right? However, more than any of the other excuses, the most powerful lie was the permission I did not realize I already gave myself to have sex by leaving room for thoughts like, *It's okay if you're in love.* How "wise" I was in my own eyes.

The summer between my junior and senior year, I took my first solo flight and returned to Florida to visit with my Satellite High friends. Florida still felt like home to me. I stayed at my friend Nikki's house. From my perspective, Nikki had dramatically changed during the one year I was away. I got to see a lot of my friends, but she had an additional network of friends that seemed to run on the wilder side—wilder to me, anyway. I leaned more toward the controlled risk-taker side of life. I had a couple of "left me breathless" type experiences, including my extremely brief experimentation with marijuana during my return visit to Florida. Drugs always made me so uncomfortable. I did not run with those kinds of crowds, and I never had the urge to "dance with the devil" in that way.

My internal fear had always been, what if I tried it and I liked it? However, I did take my first couple hits of marijuana while there though. Nikki took me to the apartment of a girl with whom I clearly picked up was not just a casual acquaintance. Entering the room was like walking into a smoker's den.

Cheech and Chong came to mind. I stuffed down the laughter, which almost bubbled up out of me when I took in the scene before me. The room was hazy from all the smoke hanging in the air. Inside, multiple people sat on multiple beds lined up all along the walls, the curtains were drawn shut, and the lighting was low.

Everyone was either already high or well on their way based on their expressions and conversations. People were passing around a large bong. I took one draw from this colossal bong, and my lungs felt as if they would burst. Later, we headed out to one of Satellite's traditional hangouts for an outside party. Cars filled the small, dirt-packed parking area near the beach.

Help me, I'm melting! I was sitting on top of someone's car trunk. Well, I was trying to stay on top of the trunk. My body kept kind of rolling and sliding out from underneath me. I did not seem capable of maintaining an upright position. This bizarre, internal vibrating sensation reverberated throughout my body.

I felt strangely disconnected. My tongue felt thick; my mouth was working to form words, and I was speaking, but it all felt outside myself. When I tried to speak or even just to close my mouth, all the muscles and skin around my jawbone felt like it twitched and spasmed. Almost like that sensation you get when you have smiled too hard and too long.

The bizarre sensations were intensified because I couldn't quite tell if any of my facial movements were visibly noticeable to everyone else or something only *felt* by me. This surrealistic state made me laugh. My laughter was derived from a strange mixture of fear, incredulity, and bemusement, which kept involuntarily rippling out of me. However, I was not enjoying this experience at all. Fear surged through me.

My brain fought for coherence. *Would it keep getting worse? Would I pass out or throw up? Was I tripping? That pot had to be laced with something else.* Oh, how I wanted to go home, go to sleep, and wake up in the morning so I did not have to keep feeling this way. That single haphazard night became the reason I avoided pot. I never wanted to put any other type of drug in my body again—another unnerving experience that anchored my hatred for feeling out of control of my mind and body. Overall, I had a wonderful time visiting with my Florida friends. I had every intention of returning to Florida next year to begin college. A whole fresh perspective on life emerged, dangling in front of my eyes like a carrot on a stick. College in Florida was right around the corner.

Upon returning to Colorado, a new outlook and attitude shined brightly on my senior year. I felt still warm and buoyed by my time in sunny Florida. Was I still transfixed by everyone's pools, sparkling and glowing in the dark, as the plane swooshed away from the bespeckled landing strips of Orlando Airport that final night? The airport images fluttered and danced tauntingly in my mind's eye, reminding me of some of my then-favorite Florida-based movie or television shows, scenes such as the original *Miami Vice* series or the movie *Band of the Hand*. Maybe I was just ready for a change. Most assuredly, the looming allure of college affected my mindset. A "start over" I actually relished for once. In fact, I was chomping at the bit to uproot again as long as it was back to Florida.

Whatever the reason, probably a combination of all of them, I made a whole new set of friends and took on a number of new opportunities to plug in during my final year of high school. I still chose not to participate in basketball or any other sport as I had in previous years. However, I eagerly participated in a number of other fun activities.

The final, closing chapter of high school brings with it all types of special "senior" events and privileges. Two of the most anticipated treats were the senior trip and senior skip day. Of course, our senior trip was snow skiing at one of the many fabulous resorts dotted around the great Rocky Mountains. Some of my fellow classmates skied before they walked.

That trip allowed me to see so many of my classmates in a completely different light, more relaxed and carefree. The guys' donned ski outfits consisting of brightly colored bandannas and shirts, even overalls and a cowboy hat. I tackled my first ski jump and Black Diamond slopes. For those not in the know, all ski slopes are color coded by degree of difficulty.

Typically, only the higher difficulty-level slopes include moguls, which are these variously sized and spaced igloo-shaped snow mounds scattered across the top end of the said slopes. Going fast is better than slow, I was told. *Hmm.* It's breathtaking to be launched skyward or to wonder when you'll face-plant into one of those little heaps of packed snow.

I truly stepped out of my comfort zone by going on this trip because I didn't know anyone all that well. Going skiing with so many classmates that I barely knew felt awkward and risky, but it was a ton of fun and a great challenge for myself. In the end, I was glad I took the plunge. However, with every high there is a low and a devastatingly unforeseen shoe was about to drop on my time at Rampart High.

Rape. Such a small four-letter word, yet, it packs a billboard sized punch. Not surprisingly, it happened at a party. I looked forward to the party because I would finally be meeting a lot of people, the "in" crowd types. I don't remember being there all that long when, at some point, I ran into Matt. He sat behind me in speech class.

He was hilarious, fun, and flirty with everyone. We used to wonder if he was bisexual because that was kind of how he presented himself. He seemed to enjoy making amorphous kind of statements intentionally phrased to cause you to tilt your head and go, "Hmm, what did he mean by that?"

He always looked stylish in his new-age rocker way. Everybody loved Matt. When I saw him at the party, we easily struck up a conversation. The party was crowded and noisy. I thought we were heading downstairs to move away from the noise, at least that was what he said. I had never been to this house before that night.

What I didn't know was this particular flight of stairs led straight to a bottom floor bedroom. The stairs were dark, and there was no light on, so I didn't realize I entered a bedroom until I was inside it, and my eyes had adjusted. The door clicked behind me. I saw him lock the door. He stood in front of the door. The bed was immediately inside the doorway to the right of the entranceway, up against the same wall. I asked, "What are you doing?"

He just wanted to talk, he responded. He showered me with kind flattery. I told him I wanted to go back to the party. "No, let's talk," I heard him say again. He wanted to tell me how much he liked me. Tim and I had broken up and were no longer an item at this point. He wanted to know what it was like to be with me, no big deal. I snorted in reaction and told him, "No." I gave him my best derisive look, and repeated that I wanted to leave. Back and forth went this twisted conversation. He remained in front of the door the whole time.

An eternity seemed to pass. At one point, I turned and walked into the master suite bathroom. I don't remember any windows in the bathroom. I stood in front of the mirror, desperately trying to control my breathing and my emotions so I could figure out how to handle this mess. *What was I going to do? Was this really happening?* I was terrified. *Should I scream? Should I pitch a fit? How could anyone possibly hear me? He wouldn't hurt me, would he?*

I thought he was one of the nice guys. I couldn't seem to get my thoughts into any form of coherence. I had no idea how to handle him. Upon leaving the bathroom, I again told him I wanted to leave and go back upstairs. I was trapped. The party was really loud, and we were all the way downstairs. The door was locked, and he was not letting me by. I finally conceded. I didn't know what else to do.

To my disgust, I resigned myself to this fate, and thought, *At least you're not a virgin anymore.* We never fully undressed. I don't remember my bottoms coming off. I only remember being on my back, with him on top, willing my brain and body to not feel a thing. I laid there and didn't move a muscle or make a sound. *This will all be over soon.*

Later, I remembered wondering if he even noticed my complete lack of involvement. When it was over, he opened the door, and we returned to the party. I slightly recall he commented that was nice or some such ridiculousness. I don't remember anything else of that night. I don't remember staying at the party after the rape. I remember looking around at all these happy, drunk faces, paranoid if it was obvious what had just happened.

No one else seemed to even be aware we were gone. I was clueless as to how long we'd been down there. I have no memory of going home. I never told a soul, not even my best friend, Dawn. I mentally compartmentalized the entire night, locked it up tight, and threw away the key. I simply focused on what was ahead. In a matter of months, I'd leave this place behind forever. I focused on what I could control, the next steps.

College was all I ever really wanted. I can't say, I knew exactly what I wanted to do for a living. I just unquestionably knew I was attending college, preferably in Florida. In one of my classes, two girls, not friends of mine, just casual acquaintances from class, asked me about my plans after graduation. I quickly exclaimed, "College in Florida." Their reaction completely stymied me.

One of the girls looked directly at me and said, "What about Tim? What will happen to your relationship if you don't stay here?" I had no idea they knew anything about Tim. At this time, Tim and I weren't together, but we were still talking, and he had started expressing an interest in attending college in Florida as well.

Almost as surprising as her question was my blurted retort, which I said a bit more forcefully and defensively than warranted. "What about Tim? He's always known I was returning to Florida for college." She just assumed we'd planned to go to college together. I assured her that if Tim and I were meant to be together, then we'd make it through college regardless of being in the same state or not.

The conversation irked me. *What a typical "girl" response, assuming "I" would drop all my plans because of a relationship*, I thought to myself. My life doesn't revolve around a guy. I was following my dreams, period. I had already been countering Tim's desire to go to Florida.

To me, it was a mistake for him to change his plans just because of me. He had never talked about college in Florida until my departure became more imminent. I didn't know it at the time, but the Lord was severing some important emotional ties to Colorado. Tim was the first. Next, was my best friend, Dawn.

Dawn and I formed a fast friendship during our last year in high school. However, she wasn't exactly the most positive influence in my life. She had an infectious laugh, a larger-than-life type of personality and a breathtaking body. We were practically joined at the hip our senior year. She was my first true best friend with whom I shared deeply and in whom I confided my heart and soul.

It didn't take long to learn she was a manipulator. However, I rationalized her behavior as just that freewheeling, "devil may care" part of her personality. I dismissed her tactics as careless or airheaded but never as intentionally harmful to me. I allowed myself to be blinded by her charisma, which colored all her actions in my eyes. In fairness, I secretly wanted to prove to myself, I could be just as daring as her.

Truth be told, my mind was at war with itself. I failed to recognize it as a spiritual battle. Instead, in my mind, I was simply challenging myself to be more outgoing and spontaneous. I was always so cautious and logical but inwardly desired to be free of such constraints, at least some of the time. Why did I just get a flash image of Eve and the tree of knowledge of good and evil? Oh, yes, because I was replacing what I knew to be right with my own version of "sounds good to me."

As the year closed out, Dawn began talking more about being jealous I was going to Florida, fulfilling my dreams and plans. We planned a final night together just prior to the date my dad and I would be driving for my freshmen orientation at the University of South Florida in Tampa, Florida.

It was our typical foursome: me, Dawn, Jay, and Casey. Jay was my guy best friend. He was charming, cute, vulnerable, and a ton of fun. I loved Jay to pieces. Dawn was to pick me up that night to meet up with Jay and Casey for my send-off. She never showed up. This was before cell phones.

As soon as she was late, I knew she wasn't coming. The strength of the conviction surprised me because, mentally, I was trying to leave room for, "She's just late. She wouldn't do this," but I knew. I waited for hours, hoping against hope she would show up or call. Jay didn't call either. I fumed and paced in my room.

I inherently suspected she'd pull a no-show stunt, but that didn't lessen the sting. Not hearing from Jay shook me even deeper. *No big deal. I'm leaving soon anyway.* Desperately, I tried and failed to stuff my emotions into another mental box to lock away. Instead, I tossed and turned all night. Then everything changed.

The sound of blood rushed through my ears. My heart thudded against my chest. My ragged breath sucked in the air around me in great gasps as my brain fought to orient itself. It was a little after 1:00 a.m. I sat bolt upright in bed.

Echoes of the voice in my head still resounded with, "*That's exactly what she told them.*" I'd had a dream, a vision. I saw Dawn, Jay, and Casey together. I heard her remark that *I* had changed my mind about going. She claimed I couldn't handle saying goodbye. Jay countered with that being completely unlike me, especially not to have called him.

Dawn essentially convinced them both that I didn't want a long, drawn-out, emotional farewell from everyone. Plain as day, I visually saw and audibly heard the entire conversation. I was in the room, hovering above them. Instinctively, I knew it was true as I tried to recover my equilibrium. The vision explained why I didn't hear from Jay, why Dawn bailed on me, and why it had happened. I slept surprisingly sound afterward.

Jay called me the next afternoon, wanting to know why I didn't show up, why I didn't call, what happened, and what was going on. Relief flooded through me. *I knew it* flashed like a banner through my brain. So I told him. Dawn never picked me up. She never called. Nothing. She simply did not show up.

Jay went off. He knew I would never do anything like that. He knew Dawn had to be lying. He told me the whole conversation he and Casey had with Dawn that night. Curiosity getting the better of me, I asked Jay when they had this conversation. It was the precise time I awoke from that vision and sat up in bed.

My jaw dropped open. Excitedly, I told Jay all about the vision I had about them. We apologized to each other for allowing Dawn to get in between and being too prideful to call each other directly last night. It was why he was calling now; it was just eating at him.

Dawn apologized to me eventually as well. She admitted she was jealous I was going to Florida. She had always talked about doing the same but just could not leave home in the end. God graciously allowed me to still see both Jay and Casey separately before I left for Florida where I was further blessed by their special personal farewell gifts. God is so good.

2

Boxcars of Milestones

Tears shed, tight hugs, too much luggage in hand, I turned to face all the newer campus dorm buildings of the University of South Florida—destination college reached. My soon to be actualized adulthood was finally preparing for launch. I was only seventeen years old for the first month and a half of my college freshman year. I fully embraced all awaiting new opportunities, new challenges, new friends, and a new lease on life.

Nary a soul did I know upon arrival at USF. Clothed in minty-fresh boldness, I acted on an invisible kick from behind and approached a random girl, Erin—cold, no mutual friend's introduction, and no excuse in existence. She didn't appear to have come with anyone. I had arrived alone at a meet-and-greet dorm floor party.

Erin sat on the edge of a wall-attached desk in one of the dorm suite areas, casually talking with someone standing next to her. In USF's newer dorm buildings, like mine, there were two dorm rooms, two people bunked per room with a shared closed-in common area, which included four desks as well as a shared bathroom.

Erin exuded an easy coolness, and I loved the way she dressed. I mentioned the way we met because I was still battling past my inherent introverted tendencies. Shutting down all my self-doubt, fears, and anxieties, I made myself go to that party so I could meet people. So when I saw her sitting there, I forced myself to walk over to her and introduce myself. She became one of the first friends I made in college. See, I just needed to will my emotions into obedience and look what good things can happen.

Joanne, Tracey, Erin, and I became a fast knit fearsome foursome. Joanne and Tracey both lived on my dorm floor, while Erin lived in a different dorm. We all instantaneously clicked. Breakfast, lunch, dinner, everything in between, and every night, we did virtually everything together that first year. They even threw me a party for my eighteenth birthday.

Did I run from Christ in college? Certainly, I would have never believed that was true. I wasn't tethered to the Word of God or my faith. I never even comprehended I was adrift in the winds, being buffeted to and fro by the world's perspective on everything. Blind to the deceptive wiles of the enemy in my life, and without even realizing it, I had replaced my views with Christ's view and decided there was no need for Christian friends or activities. *I am a Christian,* I piously championed to myself.

A statement that amounted to a hill of beans because my roots were so shallow, they were barely covered over by dirt. Little did I appreciate how my past Christian school experiences played into the reasonableness of believing I wouldn't meet anyone to whom I could relate or with whom I could feel a true connection.

But therein lies the problem: I was at the center of my thinking instead of Christ. So everything in college revolved around excelling in classes, parties, friendships, and two more long-term relationships. Both of those boyfriends cost me dearly.

Naively fueled by the freedom found in college to, at least, feel all grown up, I once again found myself exclusively dating someone my freshman year, John. Erin dated one of John's closest friends, Rick. Between John's cadre and ours, we went out regularly as a group. Maybe, in part, this interconnection of lives sealed a bond with John that otherwise might not have been as tight. We dated my entire freshman school year and summer.

Erin and I had planned to move in together for our sophomore year. She helped me get a good-paying job in Washington DC, right outside Springfield, Virginia, where her family lived so we could earn money to furnish our apartment. We worked the majority of the summer. I flew from DC to Chicago to see John before flying back to Florida to start my second year of college.

I met his parents and brother, who all lived on a golf course outside Chicago. I was in for quite a shock with his mother. *Uh-oh, John's mother just asked me to lunch privately with her?* Instinctively, I had a sneaky suspicion why. John didn't seem to give it a second thought. I should've been just as clueless as John, but I knew exactly the reason.

Holy Spirit was trying to gain my attention. John wanted to marry me. He discussed it with me and shared he saw things heading that way between us. I did not. Weird, right? As with Tim, I truly believed marriage was for later, after college, not during.

My visit was not a "meet the parents" moment, nor did I have any knowledge or expectation that he said anything to his parents of his intentions. It was simply a visit before school began again. At our lunch, she proceeded to let me know that John had goals and things to accomplish, and she didn't want anything slowing down or interfering with his plans.

Even though I suspected this would be what she'd say, I was still flabbergasted. I was also incensed. It took every fiber of my being to control my facial expressions and my tone once I spoke. Calmly, I informed her that I also had every intention and goal for completing college and pursuing a career for myself. I had no plans to get or to be married before such time, and John was well aware of my feelings on the matter.

His mother reflected aplomb but couldn't entirely hide her surprise at my words. I was exceedingly curious to know, had John said something to his mother for her to feel so compelled to attempt to thwart our relationship? Did she act on her own?—either way, the sheer gall of it all.

I could barely get my head around the fact that we were actually having this conversation. I never told John. Somehow, it seemed that no matter how carefully I chose my words or described things, it would just come out wrong or be taken wrong. Radical change was coming to my and John's relationship.

Don't touch me. I don't want you anywhere near me were the first thoughts in my head when I saw John standing at the top of the spiral staircase of my new apartment. My sophomore year hadn't even started yet. I had just sat down on the couch when I realized I could hear sound upstairs. I knew Erin wasn't home. Alarm bells loudly clanged in my head as I tried to make sense of what I was hearing.

Erin never said she let someone in. John came to the top of the stairs. Erin had let John and Wade borrow our shower when they got into town because they couldn't get back into their own dorm rooms yet. The first sight of John hit me with the force of a two-by-four. Anger, fear, and confusion simultaneously ran through me. Why was I feeling such strong emotions?

I didn't know the Holy Spirit was at work again, preparing me for a major change. Later, I confided in Erin. I knew my relationship with John had to end, but I didn't completely understand why. The emotions and prompting were so intensely strong. I broke up with John within a week or two of that experience. Everything went downhill from there. Understandably, he was more confused and shocked than me at this abrupt breakup.

For the remainder of the semester, he showed up before my classes, after my classes, and in between my classes. He called me in the morning, during the day, and in the wee hours of the night. He called all my girlfriends, seeking an explanation he could accept for our breaking up. I tried being understanding and explaining myself best I could. Eventually, I became downright rude and cruel in an all-out effort to appease him and stop his behavior.

On top of his constant stalking, I had classes all day, two days a week, from 8:00 a.m. to 9:00 p.m., worked every other day of the week, went out virtually every night, and studied like a fiend every other available hour of the day or night. I'd come home at 1:00 or 2:00 a.m., whether from going out or studying, get up at 6:00 a.m., and start all over again.

John cheated on me? Late one night, I wept in Erin's bed after he finally admitted his obsessive behavior was because he cheated on me over the summer. Erin knew. Her words stopped me cold. She had warned him that he had two weeks to tell me, or she would. Almost instantly, I sat upright in her bed. My tears went from streaming unheeded down my cheeks to stopping as quickly as closing off a water spigot.

She inadvertently confirmed what only the Holy Spirit understood. I had been starting to feel guilty that I overreacted or something, but in that moment, confirmation struck its chord. That's what I picked up on from him and just never knew it. His cheating was the reason he went all psychotic on me. He had never lost at anything before. He admitted it drove him crazy I ended things before I learned he cheated, and now he couldn't make things right.

Later, Erin told me how unnerved she was by my sudden withdrawal of all emotions that night. The suddenness of my reaction startled even me. Erin had no way to know how strong and powerful the clarity to end the relationship hit me, nor could she understand how her confessed knowledge transferred the emotion into rock-solid conviction the relationship was over.

Total mental and physical exhaustion was the fallout from such an out-of-control conclusion to that relationship. I had maintained an intense work-and-school schedule, and the stress of John's stalking behavior took its toll on me. I was burned out by the end of that first semester of my sophomore year. Upon returning to Colorado for Christmas with my family, I collapsed.

For the entire first week at home, I could not get out of bed literally. It felt like lifting concrete to open my eyes and like climbing Mt. Everest to lift my body erect while still in bed. I could only be awake for fifteen minutes at a time before zombie walking back into my bedroom and dropping like a sack of potatoes into my bed. Needless to say, my parents were gravely alarmed. They had never witnessed anything like this before, and they were scared for me. This pathetic routine continued for a solid seven days when my dad resolutely determined to get me to the Air Force base doctor for an explanation or solution, anything.

What was the learned doctor's answer? Stress. It was just stress. My dad's jaw dropped open, abruptly closed, and his jaw muscle twitched and moved before he blurted, "Stress! It can't be just stress. She can't get out of bed. She can barely sit up."

"Stress," the doctor repeated, "college is stressful."

My dad's ears were flaming hot, Cheeto red.

Boy, was my dad mad. I thought my mild-mannered father just might make a lunge for this doctor; he was so incensed. My heart sank, but I was so weak and fatigued; I barely cared. I needed my bed. Due to my health and for the benefit of improving my state of mind, I did not return to Florida the second half of my sophomore year.

I struggled intensely with the decision because it made me feel like I was "throwing in the towel," and I am not a quitter. In the end, I knew that I needed to stay away from John and Florida, at least for now. My health and energy returned at a painstakingly slow pace but eventually normalized. In the end, I remained in Colorado and attended University of Colorado at Colorado Springs (UCCS) for one semester, returning to USF for my junior year.

Shortly into my junior year, I started my next long-term relationship with Greg, which ended in near-disastrous fallout for all my hopes and dreams up to that point. As a criminology major, my main interests were law school or a federal agency, such as the Drug Enforcement Agency (DEA) or the Federal Bureau of Investigation (FBI). I learned about a cooperative program at USF, whereby if accepted, I would intern with, say the DEA, for a semester and then return to school for a semester and repeat that cycle again.

The program had just reopened, and I could just satisfy the requirements if I started as soon as possible. I was tentatively approved when hiring freezes, for all the federal agencies hit nationwide, and the program went on hold. In the interim, Greg, who I'd been dating for about six months, got arrested by the ATF for attempting to sell a converted semiautomatic into a fully automatic submachine gun to an undercover agent.

"Will you accept this call?" the mechanical voice inquired. The color drained from my face, and my body went numb as I heard Greg ask if I could pay his bail so he can get out of jail. This phone call was how I learned of his arrest. I was standing at the receptionist desk of the law firm where I worked as a legal runner and fill-in receptionist, in the heart of downtown Tampa, when his collect call from jail came in.

Stupefied doesn't even begin to cover what I felt in that moment. Barely aware of asking someone to cover for me, I aimlessly wandered into the office manager's office. My mind was reeling. I could barely breathe. *This isn't happening. This isn't happening,* I uselessly repeated to myself. Of course, my office manager, who was wonderfully empathetic, didn't know what to say either. I couldn't afford the bail, so he had to stay in jail.

Then, like a kick to the stomach, I remembered, I was supposed to start this co-op program with the DEA soon. What if they found out? Was I required to say something? The interview process had been pretty intense; they scrutinized every detail of your life. Feeling overwhelmingly compelled, I called the agent in charge. No one else I asked seemed to think it was necessary or required.

"We know. You're lucky you called because we already knew" were the first words out of the agent's mouth when we spoke. I was utterly speechless as he explained how they knew. Graciously, he informed me that it said a lot about me that I initiated the call. He assured me that my spot was still secure because I did call. He made it crystal clear that would not have been the case if they had been forced to contact me.

Naturally, I was interviewed by the ATF regarding Greg's arrest. Erin went with me as moral support. Meeting with the agents was nerve-racking and somehow ridiculous all at the same time. How? The agents made the patently absurd accusation that Greg was some high-level gun dealer based, apparently, on his depth of knowledge about weapons and the fact *he* modified the weapon. Now, while this was not an unexpected tactic of such interviews, it was just laughable in Greg's case.

My surprisingly glib response was, "You're joking, right? You guys have seen where he lives, how little he has in the way of worldly goods, not even a car, correct?" He had no money in a bank. I mean, come on, who were they fooling? I reminded them his knowledge came from his years in the civil corps and attendance at a military school. His conversion of the weapon came from a library book. One agent actually cracked a partial hint of a smile.

Granted, it was still a colossally stupid move on Greg's part to blow up his life and impact mine in such a way. Now, the cloud of what would happen to him hung over us for months. My co-op program with the DEA was up in the air because they were waiting to see what the investigation would reveal about me and what I might have known beforehand, which was zippo. He was sentenced to one year of federal lockup at a prison in Jesup, Georgia.

By God's grace, the co-op program became a nonissue for me. Because of multiple hiring freezes, I became ineligible for the program since I would graduate before I could do two cycles of internships. The emotional turmoil of the whole ordeal was gut-wrenching though. I didn't date anyone else for the remainder of my junior year or my senior year of college. I buried myself in school and work.

Greg's crime could've permanently marred my future in law enforcement or the legal profession if the agents hadn't believed me. Anger over what could've happened and how bad the fallout could've been tickled at my brain, but I refused to let it take root. Once again, I simply shut down the emotional impact and focused only on what my next steps would be for my future.

What bothered me even more though was how a simple choice, who to date, turned nearly disastrous for me. What was I doing dating? Was I still just allowing relationships to develop as opposed to being selective and thoughtful about who I gave my time to? Was I even applying any standards to my dating? What was I actually looking for in a relationship, and what traits really mattered? For the first time, I challenged myself as to why I dated non-Christians. I learned I didn't have an answer other than I used to think it didn't matter.

A season of spiritual awakening dawned sometime after Greg went to prison. Timing wise, this was near my last year of college in 1991 and before starting law school in the summer of 1992. I hadn't stepped foot inside a church, of my own accord, since leaving for college. I went with my parents whenever I returned home but not on my own.

Throughout my childhood, my parents were always very active in every church we attended. My brothers and I attended a variety of youth groups or Sunday schools, some more active and larger than others. I first asked Christ into my heart in Europe. I did it again at thirteen years old while attending a Christian camp with a friend. The preacher was an energetic "hell, fire, and brimstone" type.

I felt stirred by his sermon to ask Christ into my heart again. Maybe I needed to confess again now that I was older and knew I meant what I professed to the Lord. I actually had those thoughts. It felt like such a relief to hear my confession of faith out loud. I prayed and tried to read the Bible in my teen years but felt like I didn't really know if "I was doing it right."

The Lord tugged at my heart for some time, but he had my attention now. I was empty. I felt void but couldn't quite put my finger on what the problem was exactly. Something miraculous happened once I was on my own. Granted, I had been "on my own" all through college in the sense of being separated from my family.

At this time though, I was focused on a career. I lived alone in my own apartment. I worked full-time and paid all my own bills. What changed? I was more fully stepped into my adult life. I felt the weight of life decisions and of my future. Something was missing though. On what felt like a whim but was actually conviction, I decided to find a church.

All by my little lonesome, I started visiting churches. Sitting inside this one church, as I listened to the sermon, tears rolled down my cheeks. The pastor spoke a message tailored directly for me. It seemed as if he could see right into the emptiness of my soul. God graciously prompted a woman to walk over to me and ask if everything was all right. She handed me a tissue.

I explained, I wasn't even sure why I was crying. You know what she said to me? She said, that's the Holy Spirit moving in your heart. *Say what?* Her name was Bonnie, and she invited me to her Joy Circle, which was what they called women's life groups. To this day, that God-ordained meeting remains one of the most beautiful gifts I ever received from him. Christ demonstrated that every step of my obedience opened another blessing.

Bonnie's obedience to Holy Spirit opened the door for me to tip that first toe deep into the nourishing waters of the power for growth whenever in the company of Christ-seeking believers. These ladies changed and shaped my early nibbling into my own personal faith with Christ. That's what the void was all about. I slowly realized, those feelings and struggles with this constant sense of inner restlessness were due to a lack of closeness to Christ.

I came face-to-face with understanding that I had no personal, real, working relationship with him of my own apart from my family. I was very driven and ambitious, and all I really wanted was to go to college and start a career. In my mind, faith, marriage, and family just came later. In fact, I was so dismissive of marriage and family; I feared I would end up being one of *those women.*

The type of woman so driven, she never gets around to marriage and family or, at the very least, if married, not prioritizing her kids and family over work responsibilities. I thank God that he took care of that fear for me.

Only Christ can take the oddest mishmash of women and blend them into a cohesive single-beating heart for him. From the outside looking in, there is no reason we should have all gotten along as well as we did. At this time, I was only twenty-one or twenty-two years of age. Bonnie was the next youngest in her early thirties. Everyone else ranged from mid to late thirties, forties, one in her fifties, and even one in her eighties. Some worked outside the home. Others had never worked. One had been divorced and currently single, and one was a widow. I learned so much from these women about how they each made different decisions about working outside the home, careers, children, and splitting of household responsibilities. Life was not a one-size fits-all scenario after all.

You'd think we grew up together for as close as we all got to one another. I felt fully embraced and accepted by these ladies. My faith in Christ grew tremendously during my years with them. We even went on an overnight retreat together and laughed and shared like high schoolers; it was beautiful. I devoured God's Word and the studies we did together. We prayed and shared our lives with one another. God began to illuminate to me how far my thinking and life had truly wandered from him, which led to some dramatic changes in my life.

"If you're smart enough to get into law school, do that first. You can always come back to us afterward." Those were the words the DEA recruiter said to me during my first interview with the agency. It felt like a slap only because, in that instance, I knew he was right. His words convicted me that law school *was* the course I needed to take first.

I had started waffling over whether to fully commit to law school or work first. Working for the FBI or the DEA had been a long-term desire of mine. I was living in St. Petersburg, Florida, with one of my coworkers from the same law firm I worked for during college. Eventually, I moved out on my own, closer to Stetson University College of Law, located in another part of St. Petersburg.

I was still on spiritual milk as I commenced law school in the summer of 1992. The school actually required you not to work during your first year in law school due to the high demands and workload. The first year is brutal since it's intentionally designed to weed out anyone who can't handle the abuse. Whenever someone asked me whether or not they should attend law school, I told them, "Make sure you really want it because it is not for the faint of heart. It causes the sacrifice of many other things."

My other favorite saying was, "If I had known had intense law school was going to be, I wouldn't have studied nearly as hard as I did in college." I thought I knew how to study. I thought I knew how to be disciplined. Law school took both of those things to a whole new level. The name of the game is overload—intentional work overload.

I started in the summer, so my classes were further condensed. I'd have one hundred pages to read just for one of my classes that would be due almost each day plus briefing cases. To brief cases, it meant reading the case and then analyzing and summarizing each one into a specific format. My entering class also was the last year of two of Stetson's most notable Socratic-method professors, of which my torts professor was one.

What is the Socratic method? Stump the chump. Well, it's actually defined as "asking and answering questions to stimulate critical thinking and to draw out ideas and underlying presuppositions," but in reality, it's aimed at parting the "chaff from the wheat." It's meant to make you squirm, feel uncomfortable, and to think on your feet.

My torts professor asked me to stand up, turn to a specific page in our book, and read some paragraphs. He then asked me to tell him what I thought about what I just read out loud to the class. I kid you not, the silence that fell over the classroom was audible. It was not part of our reading and had nothing to do with any of the voluminous cases I had briefed per our homework assignment.

I summarized what I read. And whenever he asked something I didn't know, I simply said, "I don't know." He actually cracked a smile, and he rarely expressed any emotion. He then thanked me for not acting like a know-it-all because you won't always have the answers for your clients either. He was simply looking to see how I handled this on-the-spot exchange.

Through the Joy Circle, Christ reshaped my perspective on education. I loved school, and I loved learning, but I no longer had academics on a pedestal. Christ challenged me to see school as a means to an end, his endgame. My outlook became one of enjoy the process, take from it what you can, and leave the striving, accomplishment, and accolades behind. I no longer desired to be as I was in college, always focused on building my résumé.

I didn't realize how this change in outlook effected my decisions until a friend asked me an innocent question, "Why haven't you gotten all caught up in the shenanigans?" He was referring to students who intentionally hampered their fellow students' success with projects or preparing for tests by hiding books, refusing to timely return books, or outright stealing and other sabotage tactics.

Shocked was my immediate reaction because, until he said something to me, I realized I hadn't been impacted by any of it. I responded that I simply never gave it any mental energy. I focused on how to get what I needed, period. If I couldn't find a resource, I hunted all over until I found it, or I shifted gears toward another angle of the same topic. To me, it was an enormous waste of time to focus on who did what to whom and why.

I never even realized the extent to which such petty ploys had been going on the entire semester—a sign of God's protection I should've recognized as such. In college, to find out someone was intentionally trying to prevent me from getting the best grade possible in the class or on a project would've irked my soul to no end. Another sign God was radically changing the motivations of my heart was when I finally traveled to Africa.

I dreamed of Africa. Since I was a little girl, I had wanted to travel all over that great continent into countries like Egypt, Tanzania, the Congo (now Zaire), and South Africa. The summer before my last semester in law school, through a study abroad program, I flew to Kenya. I yearned to take the opportunity during college. I even looked into it numerous times, but I denied the chance to myself because it seemed such a frivolous thing to do. Wouldn't I use my time more wisely by working or finding some résumé-worthy opportunity?

I was so driven by my goals and sense of accomplishment; I refused to allow myself to enjoy the fulfillment of a lifelong dream, a once in a lifetime opportunity. Now that I was in law school, I knew, without question, if I didn't go this time, I'd regret it for the rest of my life. "Life is short. This is your last shot. How can you pass it up?" I kept chanting to myself. Plus, once I found out it cost the same amount whether I spent the summer semester in Kenya or at Stetson, I was going. No brainer there.

Where do I begin to describe this most incredible place filled with such raw, untouched beauty of nature; abject poverty; rich, vibrant cultures, people, and food; wealth; tumultuous political upheaval; and death? I could just gush at the mouth over every good, bad, and in-between moment of traveling to and traveling within Africa. It was truly an unforgettable, life-altering experience. Africa almost became my burial ground.

We received a break in the middle of the summer term where you were allowed to travel. I took advantage of that in a big way. Half the adventure, mishaps, and surprising opportunities I encountered was getting from Nairobi, Kenya, to Victoria Falls, Zimbabwe. Transportation routes and vehicles were kind of a hodgepodge of trouble. But there was real danger lying ahead once me and my friends arrived in Zimbabwe.

During a guided canoe safari, a hippopotamus splashed into the river and closed the distance to our canoe so quickly; we almost didn't outpace him. We were sternly warned that they are the most dangerous animal on a safari, and they attack the canoes as a threat to their territory. During the same canoe safari, a bull elephant stamped and charged our canoe because he didn't like how close we had drifted toward his herd gathered along the shoreline. Then we went white water rafting in the Zambezi River.

The Zambezi River is rated as a class five river, the second highest on the classification scale and means difficult and very violent rapids and difficult rescue conditions. This was my first time ever attempting rapids. Seasoned veterans told me I was insane to do this river as a virgin. During your training, you learn that 99 percent of the time, when you fall out of the raft, it will be next to or underneath the raft. Only 1 percent of the time are you tossed away from the boat, and then the safety kayakers come to your rescue. What could go wrong? One percenter, all the way. We entered the class 4 rapid named the Washing Machine, rowing furiously, and then, in an instant, all went black and very cold. I popped out of the water by the time my brain registered I was in the water. My peripheral vision glimpsed our raft far away from me. Waves hit me from opposite directions, dunking me underwater, and popping me up before slapping me back down. I gasped for air but sucked in more water than air every time I surfaced.

The air was being strangled from my lungs. I realized a kayaker was behind me, trying to grab my life jacket but to no avail. Suddenly, I was flung onto the top of the kayak, but the next wave ripped it out of my arms. I plunged back into the blackness. I still hadn't taken a full breath. By the third failed attempt by the kayaker, I thought, *This is it.* School flashed into my mind, memories, and images. The words punctuated into my brain, *You cannot die in this river. You have one semester of law school left.*

Without warning, I felt a fierce yank on my life jacket. My rescuer slammed me onto his kayak and screamed, "Hold on, and don't let go!" My immediate thought was, *I wasn't exactly letting go on purpose.* I clung to that kayak like it was a second layer of skin. He took me to my raft. My raft guide pulled me up, held me up to his face, and yelled, "Are you okay?"

"Yes," I mumbled.

"Good, because we have another rapid coming." He handed me my oar, and I went back to rowing furiously. Pictures later proved, a wave catapulted me over the head of my friend rowing across from me, on the opposite side of the raft. In hindsight, I was grateful I never had a chance to dwell on what happened right afterward. I would've been too afraid to tackle the remaining adventures.

My near death occurred right toward the beginning of our rafting trip. We had to traverse the rest of the river and climb 750 feet straight up the side of the cliff to return to our bus. Then we went to the bridge at Victoria Falls, where I swan dived off the bridge, completing the world's longest bungee jump, 111 meters or 364 feet. I only allowed myself the briefest time, right after being hauled back into the raft, where terror snatched at my heart, and my mind went, *Holy shit, I thought my life was over!*

It took one of my friends' mother to alert me to what I looked like to everyone else. His mother was a lawyer in the states and had flown to Africa to be able to travel with her son, which was pretty cool. She was with us when we rafted, both her and her son also fell out of the raft, and when we bungee jumped. After my swan dive, she came right into my personal space, looked me square in the eyes, and asked, "Is there anything that scares you? When they pulled you in that raft, your face didn't look scared. You looked almost calm. And now, you leaped off that bridge like it was nothing."

I was stunned, but she made me laugh. I responded with, "Well, rafting was much scarier. With this, if three safety backup systems all failed at the same time, I guess I was meant to die today."

"Are you afraid of anything?"

I paused and told her, "Yes, I'm afraid to take the bar exam."

My statement made her laugh, and she said, "Oh good, now I know you are normal."

Her comments to me caused an alarm to ding in my head, which left me with this odd sensation in my belly. I had struggled with how to respond to her. She described my actions like I was fearless, and I hadn't thought of myself in that way. Then I remembered the terrified look on her face after she was snatched out of that same river and her understandably hysterical reaction when her son was pitched into the river.

Our conversation drew my attention to the stark contrast of our reactions but also to the fact of why I reacted so differently to my near drowning. My response had been automatic, not some intentional pretended show of bravery. The other reason that alert sounded was because her comments made me realize I had pushed what happened today almost completely out of my mind. My whole life could've stopped that day.

Only after lying in bed late that night did I let my mind replay the day and how easily the result could've ended in tragedy. Our raft guide's heart-wrenching story about losing his best friend and fellow guide in that same river returned to me. I refused to let the fear or tears to come along with these thoughts. I reminded myself, I did survive, so don't dwell on what didn't happen. I prayed that night. I thanked God for his amazing creation, this opportunity, and for sparing my life.

I might have buried or ignored my near-death escape, but its impact showed up in other ways. I found myself daydreaming of a different life. Maybe I could stay in Africa and work with animals or be a rafting guide or work for the United Nations. Maybe I could be one of those people that risked all to rescue others from genocide or other evils.

I challenged myself to genuinely consider if I should live more of life first. What did I really want out of life? What are my passions? What did I do that I simply enjoyed? Everything was about my future career. I even did a little research into some of these options. In the end, one semester left won the day. I was too close to graduation, and I knew I had to return. The impact followed me home.

After surviving my wild summer adventures in Africa, I graduated in December 1994. In Florida, in order to practice law, you must pass two separate tests. Basically, these tests take all the information you learned over the three years of law school and cram it into one monster final exam. First is the ethics exam, and the second portion is broken into two full days. One day covers general law and Florida law. The next day is the multistate bar exam, which is law common to all states versus the differences among states—for example, with rape or divorce statutes.

After those last two nightmare days were complete, our class went into party mode. We were in Fort Lauderdale after all. We converged on this one local spot that was the largest club I'd ever seen filled with pool tables, couches, and lounging areas and a sunken floor dance space. Music played so loud that even speaking directly into someone's ear, I could barely decipher words. The entire space was so packed with people; you were literally pressed shoulder to shoulder.

At some point, after returning from the bathroom, I found myself blankly staring all around at this teeming mass of gyrating bodies, feeling incredibly lost and alone. I felt rooted to the ground, transfixed, and suddenly profoundly sad. I became aware that I didn't realize how long I'd been standing there. *What am I doing here?* I didn't want to be there anymore. I wanted to run away, but I didn't drive. I was out of town and fatigue simply overwhelmed me.

It took all my strength to wander toward the nearest couch as I collapsed into it. I just sat there, a lone soul on my island of a couch. I didn't want to move. I didn't want to dance, which I love to do. I couldn't even focus on enjoying the music. *Why do I feel as if I want to burst into tears? What is happening to me?*

I didn't understand what I was feeling or why. I was terrified that my emotions were evident all over my face, but I didn't want anything to show, because what could I say to anyone? This was not the time to bring anyone else down. Everyone was elated and blowing off much-deserved steam and stress.

I was out of place, and I didn't belong there; that's all my brain could register at that time.

What I couldn't fully comprehend was that displacement was generated from my unrecognized attempt to live with one foot in the world and one foot with Christ. My faith was burgeoning and surfacing the conflicts and hypocrisy buried within me. *What was I doing here? Would anyone here know I believed in Christ?* This was the work of the Holy Spirit, bringing my life into alignment with God's word. It was disruptive. It was uprooting. It was disorienting.

Realignment with Christ caused distress, and he needed to do these things in my life. The Lord was redirecting my life and intentions toward his purposes and away from mine. The Lord knew that my life was getting ready to take a sharp left turn in preparation for the next part of my life on the east coast of Florida. Several major events occurred in a matter of months, which forced this new transition.

After taking the bar in February, my roommate quickly got a job. The condo we lived in together was sold in a matter of weeks. I received my bar results, and I failed. Then I was laid off from my job with the legal counsel office of the Department of Transportation because of budget constraints. I mean, someone literally watched while you packed your stuff and walked out of the building on the same day they made the announcement. Out of a job and no place to stay, I packed up my scant belongings and moved back home with my parents in Brevard County.

What am I going to do now? Fortunately for me, my parents had just returned to Florida from Colorado six months prior to my law school graduation. My life and my dreams had been completely uprooted and dumped out. Worse, I was forced to move in with my parents. I had no job. I had student loan debts that would be coming due soon. Everyone I graduated with was all leaving or already left for their new destinations. Since I failed the bar, I could not work as an attorney. I had no clue what to do but to go home and try to regroup.

Honestly, I was stunned I got as close to passing the bar exam as I did. I worked and studied, but I had also been suffering from endometriosis. I had no insurance, so the only treatment I could afford was paying for a mild pain medication, Darvocet, until I had a job with insurance coverage for the surgery I needed. I quickly recognized I was simply reading my bar exam materials, not actually studying or retaining any information. I wrestled with whether to simply delay my test until the next time slot, which would have been that summer.

I convinced myself that I had to try. After all, the material was freshest since I just graduated. I simply needed to buckle down. I constantly fell asleep while studying since it was usually afterwork and in the evenings. Eventually, I received a block of time off from work as the date for the exam drew closer. Between the distraction of the pain and the fatigue caused by the pain medication, I struggled to concentrate.

I was crushed beyond comprehension when I opened my test results. It was humiliating. Everyone knew I took the exam and was waiting for the results, so I had to answer the dreaded question, "Did you pass?" Failing also wounded my pride because I had never failed at anything up to that point.

The worst part though was the gaping hole it left in my immediate future. All the contacts and other in-roads I worked so hard to develop were utterly useless because I was in another county where I didn't know anyone or have any contacts. I knew the logical step would be to sign up to retake the exam that summer, but I had my school loans looming over my head, and my health status was still the same.

On top of all that, I was emotionally, mentally, and physically exhausted and even trying to think of retaking the exam was an emphatic "not going to happen." I felt like I had been completely slapped down by God. *What are you doing, Lord? What had been the point of all my work?* Yes, I was bruised and feeling quite sorry for myself. Nevertheless, God was working out his plan.

Did I get it all wrong, Lord? Was failing the bar exam your way of telling me that I was on the wrong track for my life? I fought a gut-wrenching battle with my pride over retaking the exam in a matter of three or four more months. I don't quit. My attitude had always been to simply look for another way up over or around any obstacle placed in my path.

In the end, I accepted the fact that I'd be *making* myself do it more than *wanting* to do it. I had to be all in or not at all. It was heartbreaking to admit to myself. I simply was not willing or capable of the sacrifices necessary to endure another round of countless hours of study and be successful when I had a half-hearted hope I would make it through. Instead, I turned my energy toward finding a job while I figured out what in the world was I going to do with my dream to be an attorney.

Door after door was slammed in my face. No one wanted to hire someone who went to school to be an attorney no matter how much I tried to focus on what qualified me for the position for which I was interviewing, if and when I got an interview. Online job tools were in their infancy compared to now and were unbelievably cumbersome and difficult to navigate. No one wanted to touch me.

How cruelly ironic that I somehow ended up being either not qualified or overqualified for everything. There was no way to avoid having to list what I'd been doing since graduating college. How do you explain a three-year gap? People told me to stop listing law school. How? What would I say I did instead that would place me into any better light in the eyes of a potential employer? Was I supposed to list the Peace Corps or backpacking through Europe or twiddling my thumbs?

Wasn't it excruciatingly painful enough to explain to people I knew that I failed the bar, but now, total strangers, my potential future employers? I felt as if I was spiraling down a drain of despair without knowing how to stem the flow. After another interview ending with "We'd love to hire you but…" I sobbed all the way home out of anger, confusion, exasperation, and exhaustion. *What am I supposed to do now, Lord?* Little did I know what the Lord had in store for me.

With massive debt from law school and undergraduate school looming, the pressure of not finding a job was taking its toll. Finally, I landed a job with the Salvation Army Domestic Violence program in Brevard County. During the interview, the executive director, Cindy Flachmeier, brainstormed with me about what she'd been wanting to do with the program. She saw my law background as perfect for that future vision.

It was truly remarkable. I'm not sure which of us was more excited. She had big ideas for the program but not much money. My starting salary was a little over $18,000. I loved this job. In essence, I functioned as a domestic violence advocate, educating all ages about the warning signs, what to do, where to seek help, the services, and help our facility provided as well as the law.

I crisscrossed the entire county, speaking inside elementary, middle and high schools, halfway houses for teens and adults, drug recovery facilities, juvenile detention centers, and in the jails for adults convicted of domestic violence. We conducted classes at our facility for teens as part of their requirements to avoid juvenile detention.

We were on the forefront of major changes happening in the area of domestic violence. I received a brand-new state certification to teach and educate the police, probation officers, nurses, doctors, and other professions as part of a push to diminish domestic violence through education as well as teach people how they can help their patients, customers, and employees seek help in a safe manner.

Our facility was the location for our county's first supervised visitation and monitored exchange program to provide a safe location for a parent to have court supervised visits with their child(ren). The program also provided parents a safe place to drop off and exchange their child(ren) without having to see one another. This was a much-desired avenue for courts and lawyers to offer in highly contentious divorces with or without allegations of abuse.

I felt my life coming back into focus through this job. Little did I know that I was getting ready to meet the man of my dreams or how much the Lord was using this job to prepare me for a new future still many, many years to come.

It was impossible to know who's the one. Sitting in my room at my parent's house one night, for the first time, I found myself praying about a future spouse. *Say what?* I was immobilized by this stunning self-admission, almost like being hit with a full-frontal assault because I realized I currently faced my truest experience of "What now?" I had graduated maybe six months ago, and my academic goals were *fini*, kaput, fulfilled.

3

Traversing Mountain Ranges

FOR ME, COLLEGE and my future career reigned supreme in my life while that "marriage and kid" thing was for just…later—later, after the school stuff. So now, I was experiencing this dawning illumination that *this* was the precise point in life I had always preached to myself was when that "marriage and kid" thing could potentially happen. With bowed head, I prayed out loud for the first time, verbalizing that I wanted and felt receptive to making room for someone in my life.

However, I wanted Christ to choose him. My previous track record spoke for itself. Going solo on making dating decisions was a forever no-fly zone for me. I prayed to have my eyes and my heart open to Christ and to keep my own fickle emotions out of the picture. That question of truly knowing I met my soulmate seemed like one of those impossible things that happen to other people but not to me.

Besides, out of those who do claim they met their soulmate, did they *rea-heh-ly*? I told my Lord that I didn't have a clue *how* I was going to know *this is the one*, but I trusted that if he had someone for me, then he'd help me to know when I met him. I didn't understand the mechanics of how that insight would occur; I just knew that if Christ placed the desire to be married within me, then he had someone for me.

I told Christ I was willing to wait as long as it took to meet "the one" he intended for me. Mind you, I had already steered clear of all relationships for about three years with the exception of a handful of dates. I knew it was bad when *both* of my *grandmothers* began questioning why I wasn't dating anyone. Within the next couple of months after that prayer, I met my soulmate. *I know, right.* Just hold on, the story gets even better.

For the first time, I began attending a Christian singles group in another local church. I was terrified and had no desire to be there, but I wanted and needed to meet more people. It was a large group, very active and involved in a variety of teachings, outings, and mission opportunities. Al and I met at that very first group I attended, where we had some opportunity to speak with one another uninterrupted.

Our first chance for an extended conversation was at a local place known as Medieval Times, which doesn't even exist anymore. Sheesh, that makes me feel old. So the inception of my love story humbly began while slowly winding through velvet-roped walkways, like regal royal guests being guided to view the chivalrous knights and their gallant steeds doing daring feats and jousting.

As the name gives away, it's a medieval-times-oriented dinner and a show. We didn't want to stop speaking to one another. My, how he unraveled my nerves every time he leaned into me so we could hear each other speak. His kind of lean was a distinct press into my shoulder. *Mm-hmm.* Signals folks, that's called signals. I'm no fool, and I knew he didn't need to touch me *every* time we spoke, but I appreciated the attention.

Afterward, he and I, along with a bunch of others from the group, went to a cool local coffee lounge with eclectic, funky furnishings. In the setting of this crazy, trendy cafe, the magical moment that set the trajectory of our relationship was minutes away. Pause for a short interlude to the remainder of our tale. I have to tell you Al's version of the "How I met your mother" story:

"You were fresh meat, and the sharks (i.e., other guys) were always circling, and I didn't want to be another one of them. If you were interested in me, then we'd find a way to speak with each other. Remember that coffee lounge? I knew what I was doing. I knew you were a catch, so I threw that lure out there. You took the bait, and I reeled you in!" *Men* (eye roll emoji face).

See, short and condensed. He always says, whether watching and listening to something on Facebook or speaking with someone, you've got three minutes. If you can't say it or explain it in three minutes, then you've lost him.

Returning to our blossoming love story in the coffee lounge, even though Al and I had been sitting together on a couch, talking for a while, when he left for the restroom, someone else plopped into his seat and remained there even after Al returned. When it was time for him to leave, Al had to walk directly past the couch I was still sitting on next to that same person who took his seat.

As he walked behind me, he gave my shoulder a light squeeze and made a point of looking directly at me as he said good night. That was it. That was the moment for both of us when we confirmed we were interested in each other. Funny how such a small, simple, nonverbal gesture could deliver such a poignant unspoken message that led to our eventual marriage. And as the saying goes, you know the rest of the story, except for the fact, Mr. and Ms. Blissfully Ecstatic *"found our soulmate"* selves hadn't yet met Mr. and Mrs. Desperately Despairing Lost, Confused, "Christ-clinging or die" selves. Oh, how my innocently ignorant former self would have wanted to cry out to that future self, "Ah, how much you don't know, you don't know when your young (dramatic heavy sigh)."

So strongly was our initial connection that, on our second date, Al told me he had been divorced for about three years. I'll never forget that moment. We were standing by the water. He had his arms wrapped around me from behind and began to tell me he needed to confess something to me. My mind seized, but I didn't say anything. I just waited.

He wanted me to know now so that, if it was an issue, we could deal with it sooner rather than later. He really liked me and wanted me to know everything. He then shared his story of his collapsed relationship and how it was what brought him to the Lord. He was raised Catholic and always prayed and went to church, but his divorce brought him fully into a personal relationship with Christ.

I surprised myself by my reaction. I didn't recoil. I didn't inwardly panic that I needed to have second thoughts about this guy. And I didn't doubt the truth of his words to me. He was raw, emotional, and honest with me. I simply turned around and hugged him. He audibly and physically shuddered and drew me tighter to him. My reaction confirmed for him, and he said it out loud to me that he knew it wasn't a mistake to tell me.

He knew the Lord challenged him to tell me. He stepped out in faith, and I confirmed the trust he placed in Christ. Later, once we were actually planning the marriage, I followed Al's lead. I felt the same compulsion to tell my papa, my mom's father, about the divorce because we wanted him to conduct the ceremony. There was never anything my papa had said or done to make me believe he would hold a divorce against Al.

I simply followed the Holy Spirit's leading to be direct and honest so, if it was an issue, we'd know. Papa never batted an eyelash. He was deeply honored we asked, and he didn't even need details about the divorce. It was a beautiful gift to Al and me to have my papa be such a special part of our wedding.

Almost two years after graduating from law school, Al and I were married on October 5, 1996. We had a short courtship. Both Al and I had been maturing in our faith walk with the Lord and were committed to being single as long as it took to meet the one Christ intended for each of us. Christ performed a miracle, as only He can, by allowing both of us to unequivocally know that we were that person for each other. Even my parents knew.

Do you know how deflating it was to inform my parents that I was getting married, and they simply looked at me and said they knew already? *Say what?* I had been forced to tell my parents before Al even formally proposed. My parents were setting travel plans for the next several upcoming months, and they were intending to be out of the country right around the time Al and I had been targeting for our wedding.

Finally, after about the third round of listening to them discuss their agenda, I said, "Well, this isn't how we thought this conversation would take place, but Al and I are talking about getting married, and that's the time frame we were considering." So much for asking for my hand in marriage, but such is life. Even Al's proposal didn't go as he planned.

Even though Al and I had discussed marriage, I had no idea he already bought my engagement ring and planned his proposal. The location of his upcoming proposal was what prevented me from guessing what he was up to: camping at nearby Wekiva Springs. Yes, camping. Al and I loved being and doing things together outdoors. I should've suspected something was up when he suggested this overnight event, but I didn't.

By dinnertime, the skies were pitch-black, and it rained in a torrential downpour. I was lying down, listening to the rain, sounding like thousands of tiny explosions beating against the tent. I wasn't feeling so well. Our tent did little more than keep the deluge from falling directly on top of me. Instead, the wetness seeped through the sides of the tent as the ground no longer absorbed what the sky dumped out. Our electricity shorted out, so we had no lights or music in the tent.

Whenever lightning flashed, I saw Al sitting outside, trying to keep the fire pit covered. He was inexplicably still trying to cook our steaks. I was dumbfounded. I kept thinking, *Al's not normally this stubborn. Why isn't he cutting his losses and taking us out to eat somewhere? Why is he still sitting out there in this rain?*

None of this was making any sense to me at all. I finally sat up and asked him what he was doing and how much longer he wanted to fight the losing battle to keep the fire going. By the time Al came into the tent with our food, I was feeling so ill; I could barely eat anything.

Al started to explain himself. He kept moving about while talking and trying to restart the radio. He shoved the sleeping bags around. He was doing all this activity while still trying to tell me something. Finally, he said, "None of this is going the way I planned!"

"You think? What is going on?"

"Hold on, I'm looking for something."

He finally explained himself, "Here, I've been out there, thinking how I'm going to salvage this night. None of it's gone the way

I planned." He flipped on a flashlight, handed me my engagement ring, and asked me to marry him. *Ding! Total light bulb moment.* Now the whole night made sense to me. The real kicker to the night? My hands were so swollen from the humidity and wetness; I could barely get my engagement ring on.

Can I say, what saucer-sized eyes you have, dear! I had told Al I had enormous debt from college and law school, but he had never seen details. The Holy Spirit really pressed it upon me to humble myself before Al so there could be absolutely no room for misunderstanding about what I owed. I cried as I handed Al the loan paperwork. Why? I felt so vulnerable, exposing myself to someone else's opinion, second-guessing decisions I made long before we ever met. Plus, would this all be okay? What would he think when he sees it for himself in black and white?

See, Al was my polar opposite with financial liabilities. Al had *zero* debt. Al's house was paid off. His car was paid off. He paid off his *one* credit card at the end of every month he had any outstanding balance. Distraught probably doesn't properly redress how the financially savvy ground shook underneath Al though.

His frugalness added to my sense of humiliation over my indebtedness. I couldn't get over how naked and bare I felt. The discomfort of the discussion reminded me that this was part of blending two lives and made me wonder about the many other ways we would find out how different or the same we were. Needless to say, we worked it through with the Lord. Plus, some straight talk from Bibi, one of Al's sisters, certainly helped him too.

Planning for a wedding, working full-time, and wedding showers sure made my head spin and time fly. Plus, we wanted to get hitched, so we navigated the premarital counseling course. The pastor of my parents' church and mine while I lived with them conducted our counseling. He was phenomenal. I had no idea how much the Bible said about sex until we addressed it.

I'll never forget; the pastor looked at us, then at Al, and said, "I don't care if she prances around in a negligee in front of you. It's you, Al, that I'm going to look at when I ask if you had sex."

I laughed out loud. Unexpected directness. One set of scriptures found in 1 Corinthians 7:4–5 (VOICE) was surprising and invaluable:

> In marriage neither the husband nor the wife should act as if his or her body is private property—your bodies now belong to one another, *and together they are whole.* So do not withhold *sex* from one another, unless both of you have agreed to devote a certain period of time to prayer. When the agreed time is over, come together again so that Satan will not tempt you when you are short on self-control.

These scripture verses, in particular, helped save my marriage. They transformed my ideas and expectations of sex prior to our nuptials. Only Christ knew what a powerful role those verses would play later in my marriage once pain crippled my body, my mind, and my desires. Finally, our wedding day arrived, and it was fantastic. My papa conducted the actual ceremony, while my pastor, the one who did our premarital counseling, officiated and signed our marriage certificate.

As the amazingly romantic person he is, my husband planned a wonderful honeymoon in the northeastern part of our country, in Vermont and Massachusetts. The explosion of reds, yellows, golds, orange, and near hot-pinkish, red-colored leaves is mesmerizing when the northeast is in its height of the fall color changes, as it was the year we got married. Pictures can't touch the glory of witnessing the colors in person. Your eyes can't believe the sharpness and intensity of all variety of shades of greens, golds, yellows, reds, and oranges that kiss the treetops for as far as the eye can see.

After our honeymoon, life resumed with life for me as a domestic violence advocate and for Al as a firefighter/EMT. One day, Al and I were fondly reminiscing about how we met and knowing God put us together when, suddenly, images of the conversation I had with my friend a few years earlier flashed staccato style through my brain. She had challenged me to write out this "What I want in a guy" list. Without warning, my inner Cheshire cat sprang out, pulling at the corners of my mouth, like a puppet with strings, displaying the tiniest curve of a mischievous smile.

My brain circuits fritzed out phrases and questions like, "No way," "Did I still have that list?" and "How would Al stack up?" I never questioned "if" Al would score well. My curious mind latched onto dying to know what might that list reveal about my God, my prayers, and my soulmate. The few things I remembered about that list was, "my man" had to love God. He needed to already know who he was and what he wanted out of life. I didn't care *what* he did for a living so long as he had specific goals for his life, was already established and settled in whatever he did do for a living, and had to be able to cook.

I hit the jackpot. Al definitely fit every one of those markers. I never did find the list again. At the time, what so profoundly struck me was how specifically the Lord answered those prayerful desires, even down to my husband's ability to cook. My humble meaning of "to cook" was literal. I joked with the Lord; he better give me someone who could cook, or our future family would starve.

God knew I needed more than someone who could use a stove but a man with actual cooking skills. Wouldn't you know it, Al was not only an amazing chef who loved to cook, he also did all the cooking at the firehouse. However, my husband's best qualities weren't even on "my man" list, qualities Al possessed that would be invaluable to me in the not-too-distant future, such as unconditional love, compassion, uncommon patience, and medical skills.

God truly showed me how he could answer prayers and gave me more than I knew I needed. These were some of the earliest years I attempted to intentionally fully align my life with God's Word. The first major issue Al and I faced together was the possibility of infertility. Al was one of those rare guys that openly expressed his truest desire was to be a father. We worried I might never become pregnant. We prayed a lot together and separately.

My endometriosis, which had plagued me during college and law school, had returned. Endometriosis can lead to scarring and immobility of reproductive organs that disrupt or interfere with the fertilization process and therefore the ability to get pregnant. Prior to our marriage, I shared this reality with him. We also addressed this issue as part of our premarital counseling.

Severe endometriosis riddled my insides, melding my uterus, in an upside-down position. I needed surgery. However, since this was a preexisting condition, my work insurance required a one-year waiting period for the surgery that *would* answer, negatively or positively, the pregnancy question. In December 1996, two months after our marriage, my ob-gyn performed a uterine suspension and vaporization on me.

It took almost exactly a year to get pregnant with our first child, Zackary. Between the time of my surgery (12/96) and the time Zackary was delivered (1/99), I had been switched to my husband's insurance, which forced me to drop my wonderful ob-gyn. Knowing he wouldn't be able to deliver our first child, a child he helped make possible, caused me to feel such profound sadness. However, in God's providence, he granted us another startling blessing upon the blessing of our healthy and safe delivery of our first child.

While still recuperating in the hospital from my son's delivery, my previous ob-gyn, the one who treated me and conducted my surgery, the one insurance forced me to discard, recognized my name on a list at the hospital somewhere and came to visit me. What a gift. God allowed me and my husband the opportunity to *personally* thank him for helping to make that moment *possible*. He was so humbled and touched. What a gracious man.

Everything about my life and Christian faith entered an entirely new phase of trusting and relying on Christ—you know, that practical part of your Christian faith, where reading the Word meets the living-it-out part of your life, all these new and major decisions to make together, incalculable opportunities to teach us how to work as a unit under Christ, the truest form of a Survivor reality show.

There are incalculable new decisions to make together in marriage and in parenting, which taught us how to work as a unit under Christ. During our first year of marriage, Al tackled paramedic school, which resulted in us rarely seeing each other. He worked a twenty-four-hour shift at work then attended his classes and clinicals during the next two days before returning to the fire department for his next shift. He studied any other time he could. He did this for a year. I worked full-time, and all cooking and household responsibilities shifted to me. Then I got a new job as an attorney.

After almost two years with the domestic violence program, Christ literally dropped my first attorney position into my lap. I had been praying about what to do about my law degree. I felt antsy that I wasn't using my degree. If I didn't use it, then it had been a waste of time and effort, wasn't it? On and on, my questions, concerns, doubts, and worry festered and frayed over the who, what, where, and when my legal career would begin.

How would it work out? Was I meant to practice? And if so, how could I be marketable since I never worked in any legal capacity for the domestic violence program? Remembering how hard it had been to find my current job left a lingering bitterness and doubt over looking for a new job. For all that wasted emotional energy, I had absolutely zero impact on the ultimate course leading to that first job. Watch how Christ made this first attorney position possible.

Some friends of my parents mentioned that a Christian attorney, Dick Jones, they knew was looking for some help. The extent of my involvement? Well, I applied, interviewed, and accepted the position. How do you like them apples? My view: I walked through the door of this new opportunity, seeing only the first true step into my legal career. God's view? He knew how best to raise our future children. He knew this was the beginning step to a whole new path. Christ alone knew a major spell of bleak "wilderness" would be entering my life, and he knew what each member of my family would need to weather this upcoming storm.

Never would I have been able to weave together everything so perfectly for what would be needed for the tapestry of my near future. Who can know the Lord's mind?

How shallow was my thinking or comprehension.

All those many earlier discussions we had about kids, how to discipline, how to divide household responsibilities, and how best to address day care took on a *whole* new meaning the moment we knew I was actually pregnant.

Christ showed off in our marriage when he honored our desire to raise our children ourselves. Twice he provided flexible attorney positions for me, which allowed Al and I to both work full-time and watch our own kids. The first time, while I was working with Dick Jones, my boss allowed me to arrange my schedule around my husband's firefighter schedule of twenty-four hours on and forty-eight hours off. I kept up with my hours and my clients via remote computer access, which provided the exact flexibility we needed.

The second time, Christ led me to a firm that had actual part-time positions. I never thought I'd see the day for that type of job as an attorney. I grew restless again, but this time, my restlessness was directed by Christ and not by my own discontent or dreamy idealized aspirations, mindlessly driving me toward something better. How could I instinctively know Christ was orchestrating a transition? Simply put, the restlessness wasn't driven by some outer discontent at work, boredom, or unhappiness, which caused me to pray and to seek change in order to gain a sense of inner peace.

I enjoyed the part-time flexibility of my job. I loved the fact that Al and I were raising our kids as opposed to sending them to day care during those precious early years of childhood. This time, I had peace in my heart. But an inner restlessness began to stir, like an undercurrent nagging for my attention. This physical sensation spurred me to pray in order to understand why I was feeling this expectancy of coming change.

What was changing for me? Without realizing it, these two part-time attorney positions opened my mind to think and feel differently about traditional law jobs. Being so directly involved with raising our kids also shifted my mental drive for career building into a secondary position or at least complementary to quality family time. Plus, my part-time pay and scheduled work hours turned into a consistent pattern of full-time hours as I worked on files at home to keep up with the quotas for my employer. Al voiced his displeasure that, if I was going to work full-time, I should at least be paid for those hours.

This one step of faith, seeking the Lord's guidance first for what this stirring up meant for me, was the first link in a long, winding chain of insights used to redirect my steps and open my mind to his prompting for change. In the past, I would have just automatically started looking for a new job. Praying allowed me to be open to God's plans instead of my own. Christ used Al to plant the idea of starting my own law firm. Al had always been interested in starting a business and had encouraged me to open my own legal practice since we began dating. Even before we met, he experimented with a couple different business ventures. Me? Not so much.

I never wanted to have my own business, fanciful dreams inspired by a movie of being some powerhouse, grotesquely successful lawyer but nothing remotely approaching a genuine desire for entrepreneurship. I always saw myself as a worker bee, not an entrepreneur, someone who wanted to just do her job well, work hard, put in long hours, and then go home at the end of the day.

I had zero interest in carrying the weight and worry of responsibility for other people's livelihoods. No guaranteed, specific sum of income by which to plan? Such a riskier way to live. No thanks. Little did I know how often I would be saying to myself, "Never say never to the Lord." Then came a conversation with my younger brother, Bryon, about his business-building interests.

After a lengthy discussion, he suggested I read an entrepreneurship book, which really helped him. What a novel idea: read on the topic and make an informed decision as opposed to just dismissing the topic that made me feel so insecure. In that moment, the Lord reminded me of the advice I gave daily to clients and attendees of the many estate planning seminars I used to conduct.

During my seminars, I encouraged others to never *assume* how things would turn out but to arm themselves with facts and then decide how best to proceed. *Duh.* I knew I needed to follow my own advice. Reading that book forced me to analyze how many of my anticipated worries and misconceptions about business were misplaced or based in outright ignorance. Christ used all these markers in my life to open my heart and my eyes to what he wanted for me next: opening my own law firm.

I still doubted though. How could this really be what the Lord wanted for me when I never wanted this for myself? Only Christ *knew* how crucial each stepping stone leading to opening a business was for learning how to follow Christ into unknown territory, testing my obedience, and preparing the financial and spiritual groundwork for even more challenging leaps of faith needed for my near-future health crisis.

Once again, Christ air-dropped me the perfectly packaged job through another random conversation with a fellow colleague. I wasn't looking for another job; I was simply researching entre-preneurship based on this prompting from the Lord. A colleague thought I would be an ideal candidate to help an estate planning and probate lawyer whose previous attorney had left without informing her or her clients. He explained a hybrid-type employment arrange-ment she offered that piqued my interest because of what Christ had been doing in my life lately.

From the moment I interviewed with Fran DeGraw, I knew this was a divinely designed partnership. The offer was to be an employee for tax and insurance purposes, but otherwise, I could function inde-pendently and develop my own clients. My paychecks would be based on a certain percentage of the money generated from working on her probate files (guaranteed income) and a larger percentage of any and all types of clients I developed separate of her (nonguaran-teed income). However, it was recognizing the spookish similarities between her practice and my first job with Dick, which screamed out, "This is the path."

They both used free educational seminars as the primary method for potential future clients. They both encouraged me to pursue sem-inars and build my own clientele. They drafted trust language and related legal documents very similarly; the document signing proce-dures were near identical as well as the integrity demonstrated to the clients. Excitement doesn't even touch the surface of the emotions I felt as I drove home from that initial interview.

Can you see how everything just described were like bricks building me a wall of security and assurance to jump into this arrangement? Yet I still doubted. Did I have what it took to build my own practice? She was offering a safety net with tremendous income growth potential, which certainly felt safer than hanging out my own shingle without support. Then the Lord dropped a couple powerful kick-in-the-pants reminders for me that catapulted me into accepting this new direction.

The first reminder was how I promised the Lord I would always be willing to step up to the plate, no matter what he asked me to do. The second was being returned to the memory of what happened when I retook the bar exam. My interest before and during law school was to be a litigation attorney, most likely criminal or connected to child abuse cases. I didn't have any interest in being a more office-type lawyer such as with estate planning and probate law.

However, while studying, I distinctly remembered thinking it strange how, all of a sudden, the statutory law for these practice areas seemed to make sense to me in a way it never had before. Mentally, I acknowledged this could be a great practice area since I lived in a retirement state like Florida. I recognized the clientele would be completely different, and I'd have a different type of control over my schedule as primarily a transactional attorney versus a litigation attorney.

I accepted the position with her in 2002, which was five years after my first official job as an attorney with Dick Jones. She was a wonderful mentor, both professionally and personally. The legal messes and chaos left in the wake of her one former attorney was almost overwhelming. Every day I put out a new fire because of some disgruntled client or neglected legal issue suddenly flaring up.

The positive flip side to that disastrous coin was, I quickly gained more hands-on experience with more complex and varied issues in one year than my colleagues with twenty-plus years of practicing law ever had to address. This reality unexpectedly placed me in a more positive light with colleagues and within my niche practice. This recognition, in turn, led to being asked to speak at Florida bar-sponsored CLE (continuing legal education) seminars and a collaborative opportunity to assist Barry Law School develop a practical probate course for its students.

My mighty God still wasn't done blessing me through my time with Atty. DeGraw. The way I handled her clients and the problems from the prior attorney quickly solidified the trust between myself and Mrs. DeGraw. So much so, by the close of our first year working together, Mrs. DeGraw made a most astonishing offer to me. She offered me the opportunity to take over her entire practice upon her retirement within the next few years. I would need to officially open my own law firm and share in her lease and other business expenses while we worked on a contractual agreement between our firms. I was speechless.

Seriously, how did that happen but for God? I didn't even want anything like this when I pursued law school. I simply followed Christ's prompting and allowed myself to be open to something I previously automatically closed off as an option. He is a personal God. He tailor-made the path he wanted me to walk in.

He had plans for me. He was strengthening my faith. Christ covered every one of my ill-fitted insecurities and qualms about business ownership and slow stepped me toward his intention: I had a law firm to open, a legal practice that would be the source for the financial resources, the insurance protection, and better control over my time, clients, and chaos needed for what was coming next. Life has a funny way of proving you have control over exactly nothing.

Starting a business was like looking at an iceberg. The surface part was the easy, visible part, such as the formation of the bare shell and legal requirements to officially function as a legitimate business. The much-larger chunk, the part *not* seen until you dive in the water, was the not-so-idiotproof challenge of navigating the CYA (i.e., cover your ass) minefield and best practices for your firm's business protocols, your staff expectations, and requirements as well as for the protection of your clients.

The day-to-day running of the firm was where head knowledge about what the law said on paper morphed into the actual practice of law. There was almost endless trial and error, even with the best preplanning, as you address problems, conflicts, and the attempt to balance the legal duty I owed to my clients, to the estate beneficiaries, and to the courts. Plus, I had to learn how to balance new stressors with my family responsibilities and how to turn off worry and my "business" head so I could disconnect, thereby preserving a healthy state of mind.

This business opportunity tuned me into how similarly my spiritual walk also mimicked that "iceberg" effect. The spiritually easy part was accepting Christ for who he is and what he did for me. The much-larger unseen part, the trial-and-error part, was how to apply what you read in the Bible to the "now what do I do" moment with everyday people and life. There were lots of things I thought I understood right up until I realized I didn't.

Fran DeGraw and I moved forward with our arrangement in an almost seamless fashion. For Al and me, we had some new boundaries to develop between our work and our personal relationship, as well as the household responsibilities. Al helped me with the monthly client billing, which developed almost a love-hate dynamic between us. We enjoyed working together because it felt like the fulfillment of one of Al's longest desires, for us to run a business together. However, our personalities clashed over his resistance to what I told him I was required to do according to the Florida bar dictates.

So goes the merry-go-round of "wash-rinse-repeat" life, which I relished in the beginning: waking at 5:00 a.m. to get to the gym, return, shower, and leave the house no later than 7:00 a.m. in order to drop off the kids at their new day care school. I arrived at work by eight o'clock and began my workday where I met with staff, reviewed files, met with clients, and attended court.

My workday included time for business marketing, conducting estate planning signings, and attending legal committees. Then I dashed off to reach the day care prior to 6:00 p.m., hugged my kids and caught up with them on the way home, cooked (on the days Al worked), fed the kids, spent time with them and Al, gave baths, tucked the kids into bed, prayed with them, and returned to business responsibilities (i.e., billing, working on files remotely, research, drafting documents, etc.) until midnight.

I crashed into bed for some sleep, showered in the morning, and repeated the cycle. My husband always pitched in whenever he wasn't on a twenty-four-hour work shift or at his second job. I loved a challenge. I saw this season of life as what it was supposed to be, or so I believed. Wasn't life supposed to be crazy busy, full, and to feel like a juggling act? I tackled everything with the same outlook: How do I go up, over, under, around, or through every good, bad, or indifferent bump in the road tossed in front of me.

My dependence on Christ definitely deepened during this stage. My marriage strengthened as well. It was such an exciting time. Wasn't I on top of the world? Wasn't this progress? Wasn't all my hard work and goals coming to fruition? The answer was undeniably yes from my perspective. However, Christ used this marital and spiritual growth to prepare me for much rockier ground where deeper roots of faith would be needed. The other shoe was getting ready to drop on my climbing career.

Detour:
The Darkside Tunnel

EVER WONDER WHAT Dorothy felt like when she woke up in Munchkin Land? Waking up in a strange and unfamiliar world where what I knew and understood seemed to be turned and twisted upside down, wondering, would I ever find my way back home? Well, I sure felt as if Christ took me down an inexplicable and mysterious yellow brick road, leading to an unknown world, a journey filled with confusion, frustration, pain, anger, and loss. "Oh my!"

My chronic health issues innocently began with headaches, which I had since at least high school. Honestly, I never thought much about them; I just got them periodically. I could take an over-the-counter pain reliever, and the headaches would leave. This time, I woke up one day, and the headaches were 24-7, literally and excruciating. The power grip increased in severity until they were completely debilitating.

My coworkers and colleagues began commenting on how tired and exhausted I looked and expressed genuine concern for my well-being. I looked awful. My eyes were rimmed with dark, black circles and bags. My skin took on this weird yellowish-grayish hue. My whole body ached, and I had zero energy. I literally hurt from the top of my head to the tip of my toes.

The worse pain was in my neck and ran the entire length of my spine. My skin hurt. It was painful to walk. It was painful to think. It was painful to sit and painful to lie down. Pain invaded every pore of my body. What in the world was happening to me? I had no idea of the crazy train ride that was picking up speed, preparing to derail my entire planned life.

Health crisis is a term I never thought would be in my vocabulary as an ambitious woman who excelled at every goal she sought after. I don't say this in a braggadocious way. This was my mindset. I was in my early thirties—healthy, active, and loving life. There was no accident, no trauma, absolutely nothing that forewarned of impending health failure, yet my body felt attacked by invisible microbes and mucous monsters, like the animated movie, *Osmosis Jones*.

I simply woke up one day, the pain was in my body, headaches ravaged my brain, and I never could fully recuperate, let alone feel rested. It just all changed one day, quite literally. My "day in the life of" scenario was now confounded by functioning while ransacked with pain and fatigue.

My new reality further taunted me because I had never had any major illness or injuries. I can remember, as a child, only two very unusual health-related incidents, but otherwise, growing up, I rarely needed to see doctors. I had always been thin and active. I loved to run. I played sports or worked out. As an adult, I became more health conscious. I loved Dr. Pepper and buffalo wings, but those were my two main vices.

Throughout 2003, the headaches and pain just worsened and worsened, eventually, becoming debilitating for thirteen years. The best word to describe the thirteen years of my health crises? Hell. It was hell physically, mentally, emotionally, and spiritually. Amid that torture, Christ somehow always dropped a sliver of hope. His presence was always there. He proved it daily.

I learned to *cling* to that hairline fracture of hope, like my life depended on it because it did. The amazing thing about Christ was he knew exactly where my road would lead, when it would end, and all the beautiful things I would have missed if I had not traveled that road with him. The question became, would I be willing and able to stay in Oz if the Lord wanted me there to learn that "there is no place like him. There is no place like him. There is no place like him?"

My life became like a whirling dervish of furtively consuming myriads of chemicals and poisons, disguised as little geometrically shaped promises, droplets of hope, cures, improvement, or better functioning, beguilingly labeled as a headache/migraine medication, blood pressure medications, and antiseizure medications, just to name a few. Each globule of unfulfilled promises and expectations caused another hairline fracture on the windshield to my soul.

Soon, these cracks chased each other, crisscrossing every conceivable path, rendering me useless and blind. What benefit is there to a windshield if I could not see through it? Some medications worked for short periods of time, but nothing stopped the onslaught of these crippling headaches. The pain moved into my neck and shoulders and even into my back. Naturally, I was not sleeping well, and fatigue compounded everything. I saw chiropractors, my primary care physician, and neurologists to no avail.

My mysterious health failure sent me exploring the elusive world of a hard-to-diagnose health condition. There was nothing specific to cure or to address beyond headaches and diffuse pain for a couple of years. Endless Google searches, patient forums, and books galore became my life. Everything and nothing fit my symptoms.

The ologist merry-go-round began to speed up. I saw neurologists, oncologists, hematologists, rheumatologists, pain management specialists, physiatrists, a neurosurgeon, physical therapists, psychiatrists, and even orthopedic doctors, chiropractors, Lyme specialists, infectious disease specialists, and acupuncturists.

With a few exceptions, I saw multiple different professionals in each category. I traveled all over Orlando, Winter Park, Tampa, Clermont, and Jacksonville, seeing doctors. We researched fibromyalgia clinics, teaching hospitals, and Shand's Hospital. Then another health field opened to me, the even more foreign world of essential oils, supplements, and other natural-healing methods. I made massive dietary changes, such as going vegan, experimenting with detox diets, Whole30, soaking grains, going to our "goat" lady for kefir and other products, drinking chlorophyll, growing a garden, growing wheatgrass and sunflower sprouts to make our own grass shots, juicing our own carrots and other fruits and vegetables, mung beans sprouts, lotions, oils, eating raw foods, salt water, caffeine, and neem powder enemas. I left no stone unturned.

To say you feel like a guinea pig barely captures the horror of seeking answers for an unexplainable decline in health. I felt like a pin cushion, like a scientific experiment. *Let's throw this at her and see if it sticks.* The chemicals and poisons I ingested in the quest to be healthy again seemed so unbelievably counterproductive. Nobody understood my nightmare unless they'd lived it. It was maddening at every level.

I wanted to be better, but I was not. I wanted to understand what was happening, but I did not. No one had any answers for me. Nothing. I wanted relief, but there was not any being offered. I wanted my life back, but I feared it would never be the same. I thought I was dying. Truly, I was. What other explanation was being provided for me? I just kept getting worse. I just kept losing more functionality and becoming weaker.

I was terrified. Now, pain tossed another pin into my real-life juggling act of life roles and responsibility by stubbornly asserting itself as a center-ring-worthy headliner for the circus my life had become. However, God's mercy was just as insistently bursting forth, unnoticed by me even then, because God had already given me the primary tool necessary to keep moving forward: my own law firm.

As an example, an acupuncture school was in the vicinity of where I worked in Winter Park, which provided me with an affordable option for something I had never done, did not believe would work, and was not covered by insurance. Between traveling to that school and back and the time on the acupuncture table, I lost a minimum of two hours, sometimes three, right in the middle of a workday. I could never have lost that many hours in a day while working for a regular law firm. I rearranged my schedule any way I needed to without concern for someone being disappointed in me or feeling as if I was letting anyone down.

Everything about what was happening was demoralizing. My pride in my dependability, work ethic, and competence was already taking a merciless beating from the black hole of my mysterious health conundrum. Adding the scrutiny of a superior would have crushed me. I guess, Christ knew what he was doing. Of course, I could not understand what he was doing at all. I was too busy constantly adjusting to what was happening to me. As the changes from my declining health forced itself further upon my life and my family's lives, my determination to halt this train wreck right in its tracks grew so fierce; I could barely pay attention to anything else outside this spiral. My life truly felt like a train wreck waiting to happen. There were so many changes, blind spots, and dead man's curves rushing at me, encapsulating me, and hurling me ever faster and deeper into pitch-black tunnels that never ended.

My well-established work and home routines were demolished, not in one fell swoop but in increments, spreading like cancer from one area to another, depleting, eroding, and destroying everything in its path. The more of my life was eaten up by my health, the more desperately I attempted to hold onto whatever "normalcy" I could.

Instead of eliminating responsibilities or obligations, I simply curbed, restricted, or altered what I already did, keeping any change to an absolute minimum. I started working more often via remote access to my office. I did not stop trying to work out, but I altered the time of day I worked out, then how long, then how many days, then the type of workout. And on and on it went. I stopped evening business commitments and passed up on opportunities I would have jumped at otherwise.

I delegated more at work. I referred to other lawyers' legal work I wanted to handle but could not because the idea of the added stress, time to research, let alone prepare, for a new practice area of law overwhelmed me. I barely had the energy to cope with what I *knew* I could do with one arm tied behind my back. Each hit to the ego simply rendered me helpless to comprehend how to stem the flow of damage. Now I was not just fighting to keep up my energy, but I was fighting to convince myself to keep battling to maintain ground.

What started happening at home totally eclipsed any adjustments affecting work. My kids were only four and three years old by the close of 2003. My second child, Kaylee, was like the Tasmanian devil, a swirling sprite of smoke and dust in temperament, compared to my son, the ever-unflappable Pepé le Pew. Sheesh, how can the Lord give you such starkly different children?

I was constantly short-tempered and irritable because of the effort and energy to stay upright and functioning, to wage war with pain, and to keep up with the most basic of tasks. Remember, I was a very task-oriented, goal-setting, type A personality. I was losing control, and I inherently knew it, although I still refused to accept that truth. There had to be something I could do. I just needed to be smarter, more efficient, more organized, stronger, something, anything…right?

I stayed at work until the last possible second before racing off to pick up the kids before the dreaded day care school deadline and rushed through our home routine so I could get back to work. Then I sat at my computer and played catchup remotely with whatever had to still be completed, reviewed, or answered before the next morning. Insomnia plagued me because I couldn't fall asleep or stay asleep due to the pulverizing pain.

My husband, Al, slowly morphed into Mr. Mom. He took over all the cooking, helped more with laundry, cleaning the house, and completing errands. He helped entertain the kids and tackled the large, weekly, fully stocked grocery store shopping. He also drove me to every doctor's appointment, which was weekly many times—truly extraordinary.

Al did all excess driving duty to my parents' house two hours away, to visit his family in Miami, picking up, and delivering our kids to sports activities or friends' houses as well as while on vacation. We eventually stopped all vacations altogether unless it was overnight or over a weekend with my parents.

My thoughtful husband tried to hire someone to help clean the house, but it so offended me; she only cleaned a couple times. What was offensive about what he did? Nothing. I was offended and angered because all I saw was my failing as a wife and mother. Her cleaning meant it was something else I could no longer do on my own. What was the alternative for cleaning? Well, things got done a lot slower and much more spread out over the course of a week.

Al's pet peeve was a dirty kitchen, so that was the primary weekly household chore for me to complete. The firehouse rule was, whoever cooked did not clean up the mess, which is how our home kitchen always operated. By knowing what mattered most to Al, I stopped stressing out about disappointing him, which allowed him to not feel stressed about a dirty kitchen. Al and I just found a way to muddle through each day and took each new adjustment in stride.

What *was* actually wrong with me? I've explained but not specified. After migraines never responded to any medication and no longer fit the bill for what was wrong with me, a spiral of diagnoses began to be added to my pain train. The first railway cars hitched to my diagnosis train started with degenerative disc disease, chronic fatigue syndrome, and fibromyalgia. *Spinal pain, degeneration—got it. Fatigue—definitely got it. Diffuse body pain—double, triple got it. Got it. Got it.* These diagnoses didn't point to a cause, and the solution seemed only to be physical therapy and every nonnarcotic drug possible.

I deeply resented these diagnoses as a catchall or the lazy way of saying "we don't really know what's wrong with you." Fibromyalgia was just coming into the forefront of the medical community. To me, it sounded like yuppie disease when you read the textbook case, which I fit. But getting labeled doesn't resolve anything. My research led me to see a neurologist.

At some point, this physician ordered an MRI of my neck and discovered an issue with the disc. He explained, it was probably the source of the headaches, but all he suggested was more nonnarcotic drugs. This confounded me. He insisted it wasn't serious enough of a narrowing of the disc to warrant surgery. My pain level greatly differed with his personal opinion.

In the interim, I still worked and had to function somehow. I was supremely disappointed with this neurologist because he left me with no options, without any further suggestions. On my own, I sought a second opinion with an orthopedic surgeon who recommended surgery. Now what?

It was mystifying how I transformed from a vibrant, ambitious, successful attorney, young wife, and mother into Mrs. Glass. Every day I felt as if I would shatter apart into a million pieces, leaving my bones pulverized into dust from the crushing pain. Every day I forced myself to visualize getting out of bed, desperately convincing myself I *could* still do this simple task. Once completed, the first, major mission for the day was accomplished. Demanding my body to remain upright and walk into the kitchen—second mission accomplished for the day. Eventually, I managed to get out the door and trek to work.

Every morning started with an hour-long pep talk to get out of bed and go to work. Well, "pep" talk isn't exactly accurate. (Gee, if I could insert ironic emoji face). These particular "pep talks" weren't exactly the upbeat motivational speech used to spur one on to great things, but it paints the correct emotional sentiment. My self-talks motivated me to get out of bed, while I pleaded with my body to please function at its most fundamental level: just movement.

My speeches went something like this: I spent about an hour screaming at myself, inside my head, while also repeating out loud to myself, "Get out of bed, Rhonda. You *really* need to get out of bed…now. You can do this. Okay, you're on your side, just drop one leg over the side of the bed, hand on the mattress, and *push* yourself upright. It's always better once you get the blood moving."

Then my diagnoses train took a hairpin curve after a funny thing happened on the way to work one day. I drove in miserable weather and in mummifying misery and pain. I cried as I drove to work. I was wracked in pain. I still had no definitive answers as to why I had such 24-7 severe pain from the tip of my head to the bottom of my feet. How had my life taken such a drastic turn without any particular trauma ever having happened to me? *What was happening to me? How did I get here? Why can't anyone tell me anything?*

As I was having these thoughts, I looked into my rearview mirror, and that tiny movement caused my whole neck to lock up. I couldn't move my neck…at all. I couldn't turn it to the left or the right. Fear seized me. I recognized, I was at the turn for my neurologist's office and headed straight to his office.

I prayed someone would be there even though it was fifteen to thirty minutes earlier than the scheduled office hours. I was desperate and terrified. Praise be to God; someone *was* there, and they let me see him immediately. What were the odds?

My distraught state, along with informing him of the orthopedic surgeon's recommendation, led to the best advice he ever gave me: go to Dr. Sawin. He informed me that the only physician I wanted touching my spine was a neurosurgeon.

He said Dr. Sawin was the best neurosurgeon and was very conservative when it came to surgery. He repeatedly and boldly claimed Dr. Sawin would not tell me anything different; surgery was not necessary at this time. My appointment with Dr. Sawin took months to get into place.

In the interim, I ended up in the emergency room, which led me to Dr. Maclay, who was a rheumatologist and internal medicine physician. She was private pay only and had carved out a niche for herself as someone who helped people with difficult to diagnose diseases. She was the first to test me for virtually everything under the sun. She truly helped me dig and explore for options and solutions.

She also felt I was a textbook case for fibromyalgia, but for my mechanical defect. She knew Dr. Sawin and confirmed he was the best surgeon for me. She was also the first physician to begin experimenting with sleep medications and narcotics to help me until my consultation with Dr. Sawin. My pain was so overwhelming; I wasn't even sure how I was getting through work except by sheer grit and determination.

Why didn't I consider a temporary reprieve from work? Well, I had my own employees now. I had this incredible opportunity to take over Mrs. DeGraw's practice upon her retirement, which granted me an instantly increased client base and name recognition that would take me years to accomplish on my own. Besides, all I needed to do was hang on a little longer. I was exploring other medical options. How could I know how many years this battle would last?

When I finally had my meeting with Dr. Sawin, what do you think he advised? Yep, surgery. I had bone grinding on bone, hence the headaches and some unknown part contributor to my other pain. No doctor could say, prior to surgery, whether eliminating the mechanical defect, the most obvious culprit for my headaches and spinal pain, would actually result in any overall body pain reduction. Even if pain was reduced, no one would say it'd be significant enough to improve my day-to-day existence. However, cervical surgery was the first step, in my mind, to a potential cure for all my pain. Hope sprung eternal.

"But its noninvasive," they said. Noninvasive, minimally invasive, whatever. What a misnomer, with either term, from a pain-reduction standpoint. I sought relief through epidural and, later, facet injections. These avenues were explored primarily to see if anything else might ease the pain prior to the surgery.

One particular physician's name was continually suggested to me for the injections, Dr. Evans Amune, who had more experience than any other similar physician. He was always fantastic with me, as was his staff, always. However, he did his injections without administering pain medication to his patients.

The reasoning for no pain medication? The only true way to know if the injection itself is working is if there is nothing else in your system to alter or lower my pain level. Clearly, pain medication would cause such an alteration. I understood and agreed with the logic. But I can't lie, it was ridiculously painful. My pain was not just in one location or even multiple isolated locations but all over.

The hope for all this poking and prodding? My treating physicians viewed the disc degeneration as the most obvious culprit causing my pain. Therefore, if the spinal pain could be reduced, then maybe the remaining bodily pain would disappear or decrease enough to make it more manageable. It seemed like a logical and rational course of action at the time.

In my mind, I doubted any of it could work. The pain was all over, but I kept saying to myself, what if they were right? What if the diffuse body pain was due primarily to, or in large part, my vertebrae issue? I had to at least try, right? Can you see why I say everything about chronic pain was maddening?

Facet injections are no joke. I love when doctors and staff look at you and say it'll be uncomfortable, pain at injection site, infection at injection site, allergic reactions—you know, the expected list of what can happen. No big deal. This procedure was nothing to worry about. Well, let me enlighten you as to what wasn't described to me to expect: tremendous additional pain.

I hurt from head to toe, twenty-four hours a day and seven days a week. My spine, on a good day, felt like someone was wrenching it from my skeletal frame. I changed into a gown and laid stomach down on a metal slab, waiting for the doctor to begin the facet injection procedure.

First, cold causes tension in the muscles due to the exertion needed to try to warm the body. Second, lying on my stomach was the single worst and most painful position for me because I had to turn my head completely to the right or left side, which caused pinches and muscle spasms in my neck. I laid there for a good twenty minutes. I couldn't get up. They had all the equipment in place and the IV in and ready.

The pain became so overwhelming; tears splashed down my face as I heaved and sobbed in silence, still waiting. The one nurse noticed when she came in to check on me and to inform me that the doctor got delayed. She was so alarmed. I could barely answer her questions. She left immediately to get his permission to provide me pain medication. He approved it and, literally, as she was preparing to inject it into the IV, he stopped her.

He looked at me. He apologized but reminded me he couldn't because it would interfere with my ability to let him know the injection was effective. I only had a certain amount of time for recovery. The pain medication would take too long to wear off, and he wouldn't know if there was an immediate effect. He needed my assessment free and clear of any relief provided by the narcotics. I was devastated.

We were looking for a 50 percent noticeable reduction in the thoracic pain from this new injection. Remember, the goal was to address referral pain while I waited for surgery. I wanted to die, and that huge needle wasn't even inserted yet. Was this really happening? Doubt. Fear. Could I even endure the procedure? I had to endure it. I had to know if it will work for me.

Was I really letting this guy insert a needle as close as possible to my spinal vertebrae in the hope it worked to kill the pain in that location? *No pain, no gain, right?* Laying on this metal surface, feeling like a slab of beef, the procedure began. Although he did numb the marked injection spot, the insertion of the needle took my breath away, feeling like some strange version of the Heimlich maneuver being performed on my back. I felt small palpating sensations seemingly taking great force to drive the needle toward its intended mark.

The pressure was so intense I feared my bones would give way. Then, as he injected the medication, a ragged moan escaped my lips as pain spread and crawled across my thoracic region. It was as if the liquid medicine was too thick, too resistant, causing it to ooze out, overflowing into unintended bodily spaces. As the needle withdrew, I audibly exhaled, feeling as if my breath returned as soon as the needle exited my body. I didn't receive the hoped-for relief I so desperately sought.

Right after the procedure, the area was numb, and the pain throughout a big chunk of my back was more deadened. But was that the lidocaine? My body felt so ravaged by everything it just went through. The spinal pain seemed to seek escape into every other cell within me. As soon as my husband and I got into the car to drive home, I told him I could never imagine doing that again. I did though. I knew I'd have to wait a certain number of weeks before being eligible to undergo another injection. I waited until the battling pain broke me again.

I couldn't bring myself to go through something like that again, but they can adjust and try for another location, so I felt I *should* allow another injection. I tracked my pain symptoms afterward as directed. I only noted minimal, isolated, and temporary improvement. The second attempt was just as awful, minimally effective, and I threw in the towel. I emphatically told my husband, "Never again."

All of this self-torture was in an effort to improve my overall quality of life with no opioids or the lowest amount of pain medication as possible. However, all I was doing was subjecting myself to more painful torture with nothing to show for it. Why was I still trying to work while enduring these tortuous treatments? To stop working meant surrendering to this invisible thing strangling my life. No way.

In the midst of these unfolding events, I made the gut-wrenching decision to walk away from Mrs. DeGraw's golden opportunity.

She was so gracious to me in our separation. She knew something was happening to me even though she didn't know the specifics of my daily medical nightmare. I took my clients and joined a large law firm, who wanted to expand its estate planning and probate branch.

My fervent belief was that removing the additional stress of running the practice and returning to a regular attorney role would help me manage the pain better. If my health continued to decline, then I had a large firm that could easily absorb my clients and service them well. So went the logic anyway. What I refused to accept was that I would have to stop working altogether. I transferred my clients to my new firm and closed my practice by the end of 2004.

I received Dr. Sawin's news only a few months after officially transferring to that big firm. I was devastated. Dr. Sawin told me to expect a minimum of six months recovery, sometimes up to a year for full healing. Now I must inform my direct boss, one of the owners of the firm, I will be taking an extended period of time off due to surgery. I honestly informed him, if I had had any clue surgery was truly a possibility, I would have simply closed my practice and sold my clients to another firm. What was the point of being hired to leave so quickly? It all felt like an enormous waste of my energy.

In Christ's amazing grace, the extra effort and exertion of transferring to a large established firm protected my clients because only Christ knew I would never be able to return to law. I was graced with a believing boss, Mr. Rulon Munns, who was so kind and understanding, when he certainly didn't need to be. He even offered me an of counsel arrangement, which would allow me an easier transition to either return to the firm if able or, if unable, to advise and assist with my clients or any client during my recovery.

The interesting thing about my cervical fusion was it wasn't supposed to be a fusion. Dr. Sawin's recommendation, due to my age and overall health, was a cervical disc replacement. As the name implies, a replacement inserts a new, healthy, artificial disc, allowing the spine to better maintain its natural curvature and fluidity of movement.

With a fusion, the permanently conjoined two or more pieces of bone together with plates and pins restricts range of motion and leads to future deterioration above and below the fusion point. I was all in for the disc replacement. I was only in my early thirties at this time, with the hopeful expectation of returning to my career and life. What was the snafu with the surgery options?

Well, when I met Dr. Sawin for the first time, he was only then undergoing the approval process for this specific type of procedure to be conducted at the hospital. Lumbar disc replacements were already approved but *not cervical* disc replacements yet. So it was schedule, wait, and hope the process would be completed quickly. It wasn't quick. Big surprise, right?

I had already been suffering and searching for solutions for almost two years by this point; what was a few more months? Pure hell, actually. Mentally, I knew it could take a long time, but I had to at least try to hold out for the replacement surgery. We rescheduled at least three times. Since no one really had any idea how much longer the approval process would take, I scheduled a regular cervical fusion for March 18, 2005, a date forever seared into my mind.

Dr. Sawin and his staff did a fantastic job for me from the initial meeting, throughout my recovery, and all my follow up appointments, which lasted for a couple years after the surgery. For the week after my surgery, I did as advised and used up the remainder of my current medication, which only lasted a few days. I filled the prescription the discharge doctor provided for 5mg of Percocet and slowly tried to use less as the days went by. When the medications were gone, I stopped. By the first weekend after my surgery, I knew something was grotesquely wrong.

Despite questioning my discharge surgeon about withdrawal and use of medication postsurgery, there was never any discussion of the potential for withdrawal, how to recognize the symptoms, or what to do if I suspected withdrawal—nothing, no discussion whatsoever. Well, I went into full-blown withdrawal.

As a working mom with three grown children, I was not prepared for a phone call from one of them, a call that I knew immediately was not good. Rhonda rarely called for help, but her voice told me she was desperate. Recently released from a neck fusion, she was home alone with her children, Kaylee and Zack, and needed help—now!

When I arrived, I found Rhonda lying on the sofa. And for the first time ever, I was really frightened for her. She looked horrible, but even through the pain, she found me the phone number of the doctor's office.

After describing her symptoms, it was identified as withdrawal. Rhonda had been given the wrong medication dosage when she left the hospital. How Rhonda functioned through the next hour trying to get prescriptions filled and helping me care for the kids, I will never know.

What I do know is, she was amazingly calm, but for me, it all felt like a blur. Underneath, I knew I was afraid she was going to die. Years later, when she was going through so much pain, I would reflect on that day and feel that was where it all started.

—Sandy Hand (mom)

It started as sleeplessness and pacing all night for multiple nights. This was not an unusual routine for me, even prior to the surgery, so at first, I did not think much about what was happening. I could only stay awake for fifteen minutes at a time before my body just literally shut down on me. I could not stand or sit up, but lying down provided no reprieve either.

Prior to the surgery, my pain increased all the time without rhyme or reason, so I initially ignored that symptom. The extremity of the fatigue heightened my alarm this time. I was used to feeling like I had 20lb bags of sand dangling from my wrists and tied to my legs as I went about my day. Withdrawal magnified the worst of every symptom, both the pain and fatigue, by 1000 percent.

I felt like someone beat me up and down my body with a two-by-four, weighed me down with bricks, and stole the air from my lungs. The exertion it took to open my eyes, sit up in bed, or stand up left me breathless. I was walking forward, shaped and moving like the hunchback of Notre Dame, only to collapse onto whatever I could next reach.

The symptoms reached an apex on a day I was home alone with my six-year-old son and four-year-old daughter. Al was at the fire department, working his normal twenty-four-hour shift. He could not just leave without permission or proper staff coverage, and his station was about an hour from our house. Fear traveled its icy fingers around my neck. *I can't watch the kids.* I couldn't even trust how long I could stay aware of my surroundings.

By God's grace, I managed to calmly call my mom in the hopes she could rescue me. I did not want her to know the terror tramping through me right then, just that I was in particularly bad shape and needed her to watch the kids. My parents lived almost two hours away. My mom immediately said, "I'm on my way." Later, I learned, she heard something in my voice that warned her to immediately come over; no questions asked.

After my mom arrived, my neurosurgeon's after-hours person confirmed I was in fact suffering from withdrawal. She informed me that appropriately weaning from my original daily dose required more time and more medication. The rage that filled me in that moment kindled and burned around the fragmented pieces of my mind as I listened to her words. Sure, I felt relief about an answer and a solution, but once again, my body felt violated to have additional suffering stacked on top of my normal felt misery. *How much does a person have to take?*

Hadn't I suffered enough already? Wasn't the surgery brutal enough? Wasn't the recovery process long and tortuous enough, without adding withdrawal to the picture? Whatever hell I was in prior to surgery didn't scratch the surface of what withdrawal did to me mentally, emotionally, and physically after the surgery. I wore a brave face for others but, in private, cried all the time.

The solution: I must go back onto Percocet to stop the free fall my body was in and to restore stability. I wanted off the stuff, *not* to be placed back on it. But I had no choice. Tears fell silently from my face as I listened to my instructions. This experience spurred a major setback for me.

There was always another hit coming; that was how I felt anyway. This surgery that held such hope and possibility for me just felt like another masked path to the pit of despair. Would this nightmare ever end? I followed my new weaning protocol and waited for my upcoming two-week follow-up with Dr. Sawin.

It took my mom almost five years before she admitted to me how watching me suffer through withdrawal impacted her. I was so moved and devastated at the same time. My mom thought I was dying. She said, in all her time as a CNA with the elderly and dealing with the death of some of her patients, she never saw someone as close to death's door as I looked that day she came to my rescue. *Whaaaat?*

If that was not a moment for me to raise my hands to my temples and use the "my mind just exploded" motion, then I do not know what would qualify. Do you know what that was like to hear from your mother, especially since I was a mother of young children in my thirties?

Are you questioning me? Are you wondering, if I was in such unrelenting pain, why would I even toy with the idea of reducing or taking less? My intention to permanently remove narcotics from my life dictated and overrode any other consideration. I was supposed to be getting better. I still believed a cause or traceable source for my pain would be found leading to a cure or a significant reduction of symptoms.

I was supposed to be looking for that elusive reduction in pain, right? Unfortunately, any potential signs of improvement were obscured by the smackdown caused by those white encapsulated medicinal discs, disguising the alter ego of a deathlike state within. During my two-week follow-up, Dr. Sawin quickly knocked back my pity party and reasserted some well-needed perspective. After answering all my questions, he looked at me and stated, in a matter-of-fact tone, "I don't think you realize how strong you are."

Dr. Sawin's words felt like a sharp slap to the face that alerted my mind to pay attention.

He continued, "I tell people the two hardest things anyone can go through is spinal surgery and withdrawal (slight pause). You went through both (slight pause) a week apart" (yet, another slight pause). His eyes never left mine as he concluded with, "How you're sitting here right now is beyond me. You don't know how strong you really are. Give yourself some credit for the fact you're here right now."

Dumbstruck...no, thunderstruck more accurately described the impact of his words. He was right. My goggles of pain obscured some powerful truths from view. I was still in "I'm drowning" mode, and Dr. Sawin's wisdom revealed I was already in survivor mode. I kept looking at how far I still had to travel, and he showed me how far I'd already run and ran well. What I heard was, "You will survive this too."

He knew I had no perspective. My poor medicine-mushed brain took a half-a-second-too-long kind of delayed reaction to realizing doc just complimented me and chastised me at the same time for failing to see the big picture. I was here even though I might feel like a shattered wreck and like throwing in the towel. Ugh! Was it that obvious to him? God used Dr. Sawin that day to speak out loud the secret despair I was carrying. He knew I didn't see what he saw and I needed to right then and there.

The shame I felt flitted briefly with the illumination I was only now realizing that hopelessness got buried under the trauma of the surgery and withdrawal, but he knew it was there the whole time. He unburied that emotion, and he placed it squarely in front of me. I couldn't look away anymore. I did want to throw in the towel. I didn't realize how low and bottomless this hole of despair felt until our conversation.

Although I had my lived experience, which was terrifying in its savagery to my body and mind, it lived in a vacuum with no context. Dr. Sawin placed that pinpoint of time into the continuum of his similarly situated surgical patients. Like a whirlwind, emotions of relief, discomfiture, shock, shame, guilt, and tears quickly flickered through me, each one rushing, one right after another, like falling dominos within me and through me. Christ used Dr. Sawin to provide me one of my fondly coined "gold nuggets" that played a pivotal role in demonstrating Christ's presence, his care, his strength, to keep going.

In hindsight, it seemed almost stupid how blind I was to the true state of my physical health, as well as the spiritual innerworkings of Christ to refuse to accept narcotics weren't leaving my life anytime soon. I followed my cervical fusion recovery protocol and waited. I was waiting to learn the impact of the surgery on my remaining bodily pain. The surgery resulted in eliminating the 24-7 migraines and significantly reducing the sliver of pain from the piano wire-taut muscles running from the base of my skull to the top of my shoulders. Another shoe was getting ready to drop.

By the summer of 2005, within six months of the surgery, we moved to Clermont. I continued my postfusion reality, and my treating physician for the past year, Dr. MacClay, retired. She functioned as my primary care physician and was the first treating doctor I trusted. Now she was leaving, and I had thirty days to find another doctor. I needed a new physician who would continue to prescribe my current narcotics while analyzing me and determining what potential new treatment options he or she might suggest.

Dr. MacClay's retirement set off a whole new firestorm of angst for me. My battle with the medical system, supposedly designed to help me, further compounded my life. Let me explain. When you are prescribed narcotics, especially through specialists like pain management, you sign these forms, agreeing to forfeit your constitutional rights to privacy of medical records and due process for investigation, if it's suspected you are doctor shopping or drug seeking.

I was required to designate one pharmacy to fill all narcotic prescriptions. Such requirements protect me as a patient from what, becoming addicted? Or from unscrupulous doctors? Or as a check to make sure I don't take them longer than truly necessary? Such a ridiculous and useless safeguard. This new reality placed *all* doctors on paranoia alert and caused many to refuse to prescribe narcotics any longer, unless under very specific circumstances.

Transferring to a new physician took an unexpected route even with my thirty-day notice letter from my previous physician. I only found two physicians who would agree to meet with me. The first said no because of the narcotics, which he knew when I made the appointment. He didn't want a new patient that he could only pre-scribe narcotics too. It invited unwanted scrutiny to his practice. So much for protecting me, instead these legal changes were creating larger barriers to treatment.

The second transition disaster—well, it was an unnecessary mess. I'll chalk it up to her youth and newness to practice. She was a local pain management doctor that dumped me because she got into a disagreement with Dr. MacClay. Apparently, she was a pain management doctor that might *only recommend narcotics* as part of an overall course of treatment but would *not* write the actual prescrip-tion. Don't ask me how that's possible, but that was her policy. They didn't specify this philosophy of practice upfront, and they never informed me, even knowing I was a new patient already on narcotics.

Infuriatingly, I learned I would have to take any recommen-dation to my new primary care physician and have him write the actual prescription. Dr. MacClay laid into her when this statement was made during the course of their consultation over me. Even more devastating was the way I found out I was being denied by this new potential treatment physician.

Their office didn't send me a denial letter or leave me a message. Their office knew about my current narcotic scrip when it was due to be refilled and that I was in transition. They blew me off, wasting precious time I needed to get a new doctor. Once pushed into a cor-ner, the receptionist admitted I was being denied as a patient because of the tiff between my doctors.

I challenged her as to why they had the practice of pawning off the scrip for exactly what happened, an easily foreseeable thing: conflict between doctors. Where did that leave any patient of hers if another physician disagreed or refused to write any medications rec-ommended by her? The receptionist had no answer for me. Why do

I have to keep dealing with all these obstacles instead of just getting better?

Stunned barely described the sheer outrage I strangled and stuffed as deep within me as possible to prevent it from escaping and wreaking havoc on anyone within visual or verbal range. Rabid panic over the idea of being plunged into withdrawal *once again* because of doctors that are supposed to help me ripped and gnawed at my memory. My stomach lurched as worry and anxiety seemed to fill me up. What was I going to do?

Mercifully, my primary care physician, who I rarely saw before my mystery malady began, agreed to temporarily write my narcotic and other prescriptions. However, he made it perfectly clear I had to find a pain management specialist.

He did lots of explaining—what could he do differently for me, all the new narcotic regulations, the DEA, and on and on. I wish any of these doctors just bluntly said, "Sorry, sis, you're out of luck, and I don't want to be Dr. Doom for you." Basically, narcotics patients were now high risk, persona non grata when your needs moved beyond that straight, acute surgery or procedure.

Early 2006 was the birth of what set me free and what imprisoned me. For all the angst and tears in transitioning to a new doctor, the Lord led me, through Al, to Dr. Nwaogwugwu (na-woog-a-woo), or Dr. N to his patients, a physiatrist. I met Dr. N in the earliest days of his new practice. He was thorough, kind, and firm. He inspired confidence. He became the second physician who looked at everything I'd already done medically and treated me accordingly and tackled the pain comprehensively.

He placed me on four medications to address four variants of pain. Only one was a narcotic, Dilaudid. He handled my therapy in house and was the first physician who advised targeted exercises, not formulaic rehab, as well as challenging but not debilitating routines. I contentedly remained with Dr. N until around 2013. The physician, treatment, and medical saga were just getting rolling.

The quest to stop the pain never ended. It filled me and consumed me. An answer had to exist. Drugs can't be the be-all and end-all solution. Do you know what I went through in the quest to find a solution other than drugs? Something, anything, that could even promise a hope that life could be better once again?

Through Dr. N., we sought answers through nerve-conduction tests, lidocaine injections, cortisone injections, facet injections, therapy, and massage to name a few. We discussed spinal decompression options, acupuncture, and chiropractic options. Dr. N was more open to alternative medicine than many other physicians and never mocked me about it as others had. I was usually seeing several health care professionals at the same time, just seeking relief, answers, and improvement. Each physician led to another physician or specialty.

What was accomplished by all this effort? Was my pain being reduced? No. Was my zombie fatigue better? No. Was I functioning better? No. Can I start and finish a conversation without blanking/spacing out? No. What about to complete a thought? Sometimes. My husband and I kept searching for answers. My parents and friends searched for and suggested answers. In fact, every one of these supposed alternatives to pain medication came at a pretty high price to me. And the worse part, the pain was almost always further exacerbated, even the more innocuous-sounding things like lidocaine and/or cortisone injections. They provided temporary reprieve, but I was limited in how many I could get during one office visit as well as how many were covered by insurance. My whole spine hurt, not just some isolated location. However, the goal became to focus on the most painful areas in my back and hopefully drop my overall pain to a more manageable level.

My spinal degenerative disc disease, fibromyalgia, and chronic fatigue were the predominant diagnoses, and treatment was geared accordingly. I paid for more than two lidocaine injections at times. There are risks to even the most innocent-seeming treatment, and I eventually had to stop these injections. Small holes or divots developed in my muscles, which was a reaction to the medicine in the injection.

This vain search for pain relief and its inevitable torture would be almost comical if not such a profoundly sad reality for myself and too many other people. Nevertheless, my diagnoses train started accelerating to full speed ahead. At this stage, I still described my pain in all of the following ways: burning, throbbing, stabbing, aching, 24-7, and incredibly intense. My skin continued to feel as if it was burning all the time.

The lightest touch to my skin or even a hug could cause me to involuntarily and reflexively recoil in pain. Additionally, I regularly suffered through the sensation of worms crawling underneath my skin, leg twitches, and spasms as well as the desire to peel off my skin. Yes, the pain made me so irrational as to *need* to believe that, if I could just rip my skin off, everything would be all better. However, Christ had a plan for even that level of misery.

Only Christ knew He prepared something unexpected to help me with my personal pain excursion: homeschooling. I'm truly in awe of all the pieces of my life Christ weaved together to convict me about homeschooling my children. What did Christ do? Christ started with baby steps and showed me nothing was impossible for him or for me.

Christ started dropping homeschooling seeds into our lives when we first seriously considered starting a family. Christ sprinkled water on that soil in the form of discussions between Al and me and through conversations with multiple women from our one church who were already homeschooling. Totally feeling like fish out of water, I couldn't relate to these women. Most never worked, and most weren't career oriented like me.

I had never thought about homeschooling. I knew absolutely nothing about the topic. I certainly failed to see how it was possible while continuing with a career. So, yes, you guessed it, I dismissed such a silly notion. *It's just not possible. It's just not realistic.* Christ kicked things up a notch after we moved to Clermont.

Christ used all variety of factors to realign my mindset toward homeschooling, factors such as my daughter's fifth birthday arriving too late to start kindergarten. The alternative of voluntary pre-K (VPK) was closed off to us because we couldn't find any VPK program to transfer Kaylee to in Clermont. My health crisis forced me to be open to at-home options. I mean, what was I supposed to do with her on the days Al worked his twenty-four-hour shift? Naturally, I wanted her time to be productive and useful.

After speaking to someone from our previous church, I took her suggestions and embarked on an at-home agenda. Christ focused me on only what needed to be done for the next year, which was making it to kindergarten at a normal public school. I spent about thirty minutes to an hour working with my daughter, building specific cognitive and motor skills as well as other basic reading and language skills to prepare her for kindergarten.

The following school year, Kaylee attended kindergarten, while Zack was in second grade. Mind you, in the interim, ping-ponging back and forth between Al and myself was this wavering sense of conviction we should homeschool. He'd agree, and then I would falter and vice versa. Finally, Christ just deluged me with water to wake me up through two life-changing events, which occurred within relatively close succession of each other. One such event involved my children.

So this is why people commit suicide, the thought struck me with the force of a lightning bolt and with the same instantaneous flash of illumination. It wasn't a question to myself, as much as a statement, like the slow dawning of a Divine insight. As usual, I'm consumed with pain 24/7 and my brain fog weighed like a thick blanket, heavy and impenetrable, smothering my mind, my thoughts and my emotions.

The slow creep of terror spread throughout me as the magnitude of that opening phrase squeezed my heart and seized my already unsettled mind. Reflecting back on that day, I get the same strange chill sensation that makes you feel so wooden inside. A moment truly frozen and so etched in my mind's eye as an almost out of body experience. I saw that day as if I'm high above my body. I'm watching me, watch my children. My brain registered it's one of those perfectly beautiful days early in the fall season.

The sun was intensely bright without a cloud in an exceptionally blue sky. I saw myself watching my six-year-old son, Zack, and my five-year-old daughter, Kaylee, racing all over our backyard playing superhero tag. Both kids are donned only in capes, underwear, and shoes. Super shoes to protect against spiders, scorpions, and snakes, oh my! My dynamic duo, with their capes flapping.

Capes which held the mystery to their superpowers, were cut out of those old, soft, fleece-type infant blankets every parent owns. Kaylee squealed with delight as her beloved big brother chased her around our backyard and purposely never quite caught up to her. I reflected on the pure, unfiltered joy projected out of my child's laughter, a sound uniquely owned only by children. A living sound radiating deep from within them which washes over you and surrounds your soul.

My heart swelled with love for them then pinched like a vise because I was not out there running around and acting silly right along with them. I was not out there. I was in my bedroom. I was filled with such a mix of emotions: anger, sadness, confusion, and hopelessness.

Abruptly, I slammed back into my own pain riddled body and my reality screamed once more at me, *"How is this your life?" "How can I keep making it through each day when all I want to do is peel my skin off!"* Once again, I'm in bed, desperately willing my pain and my sheer exhaustion to be something other than utterly excruciating, depleting and mind numbing.

In that deep desperation, Christ blessed me with the gift of watching my sweet and playful children to remind me of how much more there really was to lose. If I gave up now, I would only shift my pain to my husband and my kids, leaving them to figure out how to live with their pain for the rest of their lives. How do I model belief in Christ in all things if I could not turn to Him to keep getting through this ordeal? Christ used those peals of laughter and delight-filled fun on that gorgeous day to impel me to push myself into an upright position on my bed.

"You can do this Rhonda, put your hand down on the bed and push up," roared inside my own head. I fruitlessly demanded my body and mind to cooperate and find a way to engage with my kids. My soul felt crushed. Through gritted teeth, I practically spit out the words, *"I do not want my children's memory of me to be as an invalid who's always in bed."* The ferocity of my own emotions frightened me.

Startled by splashes of water hitting my hand, I was suddenly aware of the tears cascading effortlessly down my face. My whole body seemed incoherently detached from my conscious brain. *"How can I stay reliant on You, Jesus, when I can barely comprehend how to survive the next minute of this pain?"* *"What am I supposed to do, Lord,"* I plead for the umpteenth time. This event, this moment was a turning point. This moment was the foreshadowing of only ONE of Christ's purposes behind homeschooling—to give me another reason to force myself out of bed every day.

Christ's second "powering up" move to bring about homeschooling involved a women's Bible study at Mo Mydlo's house, not too long after moving into Clermont. We were studying *Lies Women Believe and the Truth that Sets Them Free* by Nancy Leigh DeMoss. One of the chapters was about having and raising children. God used this chapter to blossom what he already started.

As I answered the "Making It Personal" questions, Christ used a Thor-sized sledgehammer to pound home his message to me: "You will homeschool your kids. Period. End of story. Stop procrastinating." Just like that, I knew I was procrastinating. I knew what Christ laid on my heart. I knew Al sensed it and knew it too. We were afraid to face that truth because…well, it seemed patently absurd.

I left the Bible study and immediately wrote out a multi-page letter to Al. Christ opened my eyes and my soul and everything inside me flooded onto those pages. Tears freely flowed from my face, obscuring my ability to see well enough to keep writing without stopping. Christ downloaded the words to me. Every thought, feeling, and sentence seemed to simply ooze out of my pen, functioning almost like a chemical reaction, materializing invisible ink onto my paper. In total abandonment, he revealed things to me I didn't even realize I was ignoring or feeling, until I wrote out that letter.

My prayer had been for Al to not just agree to homeschool but to truly *want* to homeschool, for us to be united in the decision. Christ answered my prayer through that letter. Those Spirit-inspired words pierced straight into Al's heart. In Al's beautiful way, he gushed out how he knew too but was concerned about a negative impact on my health.

My letter helped him see we needed to step out in faith, trust Christ, and tackle one school year at a time. Wings Like Eagles

Academy was born in 2007. Oh, the untold gems that piled up for our family because of faithfully stepping up to the homeschooling plate could fill a book in and of itself. Christ's intent and impact reached far above and beyond a Christian curriculum.

His intent was to awaken a purpose-driven life within me. He knew I needed to feel useful to my family. I was still a wife and mother, regardless of what my mind, body, and soul felt like every minute of a day. Teaching filled me with joy. Reading with my kids, exploring countries and the Bible together. Being filled with fond memories from my own childhood, like how much I always loved to read, and I always loved to learn, true and fulfilling joy *in spite of* my deep suffering. I got such beautiful insight into what impassioned each of my children and how my children thought and processed information. I was awestruck at how insightful, smart, and quick to learn my children were about so many things. I felt tingly all over when God graced me with one of his many gemstone moments with my kids when I would reflect, "Wow, I would have missed this if I still worked," moments which existed only because my kids and I had daily, simple, random conversations about everything and nothing, all at the same time. The amount of time all four of us spent together as a family was another priceless jewel from Christ. The number of places we went, as well as the types of things Al and I were able to do with the kids for educational purposes and just for fun was staggering.

We read books in the trees. We explored nature every day. If not for these things, I would've been lying lifelessly in my bed, moping, feeling sorry for myself. When every millimeter of your skin, muscle, and bone seethed with pain, why would I *want* to move, causing even more pain, if I didn't absolutely have to? That was my reality.

Most amazingly, we learned (four or five) years later, Kaylee had some executive function processing issues, something in her short-term retention when she had to read, retain, remember, and imme-diately answer under pressure. Some of the specific methodologies of teaching the Charlotte Mason "way" like narration, no twaddle for reading books, copy work, teaching directly from the Bible, and sight learning versus phonetics for building reading and language skills were directly responsible for counterbalancing her brain before we knew it needed any recalibration at all.

Kaylee's kindergarten teacher literally lectured me about her apparently automatic tendency to read by sight was fine for now but would really harm her ability to keep up in a few years. Dr. Nancy T. Atkins, who conducted Kaylee's testing, confirmed phonetics was the worst method to use with Kaylee. From Dr. Atkin's viewpoint, she was simply reviewing test results with me, but I *heard confirmation* that our homeschooling was a gift from God.

> Before pain, Rhonda stayed with us about a year and a half following graduation from law school. One Saturday morning I returned home. And as I entered the living room, I see Rhonda in colorful workout clothes, moving rapidly through the paces of a lively step-exercise video. She had returned from running and was now putting the finishing touches on yet another challenging well-rounded cardio and conditioning session. Rhonda was vibrant, energetic, focused, mentally and athletically fit, upbeat, organized, and structured in all pursuits. During her time with us, she passed the Florida bar exam and maintained full-time employment with a local branch of the Salvation Army. Working in the domestic violence program, Rhonda established the Army's supervised visitation program for court-mandated individual visitation with minor children. The program was a pilot effort, becoming the Army's, and Florida's, first model program for supervised visitation. "Achiever" characterizes Rhonda before pain.
>
> During her battle with pain, to me, "struggle" best characterizes Rhonda's life during her fifteen-year battle with pain. Once vibrant, energetic, and physically fit Rhonda now struggles

to find energy to get out of bed in the morning and to remain functional for more than fifteen to thirty minutes before needing to rest. Previously focused and mentally fit Rhonda sometimes seems disoriented, struggling to find words to construct coherent thoughts and sentences that convey logical meaning in the context of her environment. On good days and bad ones, Rhonda's inherent sense of structure and purpose moves her through struggles to maintain schedules for Zack and Kaylee's homeschooling.

I watched Rhonda struggle to successfully maintain "nothing wrong with me" outward appearances for church and other meetings and gatherings. Rhonda repeatedly engaged in conversation with the unsuspecting. Only relatives and closest friends were aware of her constant inner battle with pain, struggling to put one foot in front of another in her attempt to demonstrate a "normal" life.

—Ron Hand (Dad)

My new normal—warfare and homeschooling. We moved to Clermont by the summer after my surgery in 2005. So the bulk of my recovery, as well as my continually unfolding medical saga occurred there. To me, Clermont marked my *initiation* into the special world of an unexpected personal wilderness and all its nefarious hidden and impending obstacles meant to kill, steal, and destroy me and all whom I loved.

Every minute of every day was a continual raging war against my own mind and body. Through sheer will, grit, and desperation, I fought on. Just the fact that my monstrous migraines disappeared, fed my foolish belief: "Maybe the rest of the pain will continue to decrease, maybe by a little, or a lot. Maybe it'll happen quickly or maybe slowly."

Foolish because, even then I knew, secretly locked away within my own heart was my guilt-ridden dread that the chances of suddenly getting better seemed as unlikely as suddenly getting sick seemed before it happened. I feared that whatever this was, it was going to be around awhile. Nevertheless, I was mentally boosted by that feeling, that inner hope, no matter how otherwise unrealistic and remote it may be for something to be true, it still just might be, right?

As the months turned into years, my constant, repeated questions were, "How do I heal my already grossly compromised body? How in the world would I know it was working, and how long do you try anything? What am I even doing or hoping for anymore?" The same questions plagued me regardless of whether I met with a standard medical physician or with practitioners in the world of "natural healing."

Quite honestly, many natural healing methods often sounded even more foreign and elusive with its own host of problems of ineffectiveness, experimentation, and dubious claims. Pursuing resolution for chronic health issues felt like this circle jerk of a merry-go-round spinning you so close to that brass ring of miracles you prized but left you grasping at nothing but air. Everything felt and was, in fact, absolutely overwhelming.

A ten-year anniversary, never to be forgotten—my husband has quite a romantic streak in him and surprised me with an overnight beachside getaway, near where my parents live, for our anniversary. A year and a half after my surgery, both Al and I were in desperate need of something to look forward to, as well as to get away from staring at our own four walls. My body vibrated with my all-consuming pain, but my heart felt full that my husband put the thought, energy, and money into setting up this little trip.

As I lounged on the bed, willing the storm raging within my cells to downgrade to a tropical storm warning, I heard Al say a sentence that stopped my heart cold. He said, "I don't know how you're going to feel about this…and I debated and debated…" I was looking at my husband with widened eyes and raised eyebrows, "And…?" I prompted. My husband handed me a marijuana joint.

My mouth gaped open, I looked incredulously at him, and my mind whirled with thoughts, but no words came out. My husband implored, "Say something. Are you mad?"

Looking him in the eyes, I stated, "I'm not mad. I mean, I feel kind of a mix. Part of me is happy, and part of me is upset." I was in so much pain that when I realized what I was looking at, the tears immediately welled up in my eyes—relief, blessed relief.

On the other hand, I was a bit upset. What was he thinking? Where did he get it? Did he buy it off the street? Why would he risk his job like that and his life? These were the many questions that shot through my mind upon first seeing the joint. However, just as quickly followed the upfilling of love in my heart for Al. Truly, Christ softened my heart for Al in that moment to not miss where *his* heart was in getting the joint nor to miss the vulnerability he exposed in being honest with me about what he did and why.

What was the story? Al wanted to see a smile on my face and to hear me laugh. He wanted to do something extra special for me, to find a way to bring joy and better sleep for me on this special night. He gushed on about how much he prayed that I would not be upset and would understand where he was coming from. He had turned to a friend who he knew smoked marijuana and bought the joint from him. I cried and hugged Al.

Together, we went to our ocean view balcony, sat down, and lit up. Was it a magic bullet pain killer? No. I was seething in pain and on prescription pain medication. Marijuana hit my system immediately, slapped down the pain level. My shoulders literally sagged as the taut muscles finally relaxed. I didn't even realize how much tension I was holding until I felt the physical reaction of my muscles to the marijuana. I slept better that night than I had in at least three years.

What was I supposed to do about marijuana now: keep using, stop, rare occasions, or never again? How could this be what the Lord wanted for me, for us? Al's position was the dead opposite of mine. He did not see an issue, period. Why would God care if we used what he created, with moderation, of course?

My husband does not operate in the land of extremes and excesses, which was one thing we shared. He experimented, in his younger years, with drugs a bit more than my few puffs of pot, but his career as a firefighter helped steer him clear of drug use. My position was a bit more mixed and muddled. My immediate reaction was this could not be right or what Christ would want. Was it a sin?

My next almost instantaneous thought was 1 Corinthians 6:12: "'All things are lawful for me,' but not all things are helpful. 'All things are lawful for me,' but I will not be dominated by anything." This is where I left the matter, or so I told myself. I believed that scripture, but I just felt like, *That can't be right, right?* Quite honestly, I could not cope with another heavy-feeling decision to make. I felt so depleted of will, desire, and energy.

Al made the decision for me and continued to purchase a small amount of marijuana. I had no will to fight him on it, and it was just easier for me. I was regularly drug tested so we only used it for a few days right after my monthly pain management appointment. This was our strategy to ensure the marijuana was well out of my system before the next month's appointment when I was randomly, then later, monthly, tested for nonprescribed and other illegal drugs. For now, marijuana was pushed into the recesses of the least of my concerns but would come into play again later.

The amorphous and elusive, maybe I will just start to feel better if I just start doing xyz myopia crossed over from double heading my listless locomotive to leading it with the throttle maxed out. From 2006 until 2016, the list of "whatever-ologists" and list of herbal/healthy/naturalistic grew exponentially along with its imbedded relatives of "holy-crap-itis", "nowwhat'isms" along with the always indefatigable Dr. Howmuchlonger and Dr. Howmuchworse. Every day was a battlefield. The desperation and anxiety built with nowhere to be released, except in seeking Christ. If Christ had me in this crazy place, then it was exactly where he wanted me, and I wanted the strength to persevere to the end. If Christ didn't uphold me, I simply would never have survived all I suffered between the pain, in and of itself, let alone all the treatments, false hopes, and side effects, without any significant improvement.

Whenever anyone asked, "Are you feeling better?" or "Is it/ anything working?" I simply felt like more barbed attacks from my nemesis, general pain. I would answer that my dance with the elusive concept of "better" was more akin to peeling off layers of an onion. I believed I was unwinding things, but each and every incremental step forward simply unraveled another virtually identical layer underneath.

My onion was losing layers but not a lot else was distinguishably different for my day-to-day existence and functioning. Too often, I took twice as many steps back for every apparent step forward, all the while wondering if I was imagining things and questioning how much further to peel back this layer or whether or not I should peel two layers at the same time. Or can I just change fruit, Lord?

I began judging my concept of "improvement" based upon things, such as more time out of bed than in bed, the amount of time it took to walk set distances, shortening the hours an activity would cost me in increased resting time or increased pain or both, or sustaining stamina better throughout the day. Homeschooling became another gauge for change because I eventually increased the designated school time from thirty minutes to an hour to two hours and, finally, in the latter years, four hours.

These miniscule betterments ebbed and flowed over countless years. There was no direct line or shortcut that led to "now you're healed" or "all traces are gone" or even "now every day you can do x time at x activity." All those years of searching and exploring, trial and error, ups and downs, highs and despairing lows, and wrestling my depression demons, chemicals, poking and prodding, all without any significant improvement were maddening. The worse all my symptoms got, the more desperate I felt, and the concept of "effective treatment" elusively drifted further away from me.

The inanity of it all is mind numbing. To me, the fruitlessness of your efforts to escape chronic pain is what makes it so dangerous. It's not the narcotics that cause the emergency, it's the unbearable pain. Narcotics become the bleak escape. When you can't adequately manage nonstop severe pain, understand that you are *already* free-falling without a parachute. Flashbulbs should be popping, red flags flying, and exclamation points should be lightning points in front of your eyes, warning you that a radical saving grace is needed, compelling you to reach out to anyone who will listen. *What do I do with all this pain?*

The frightening truth, all this emotional and physical angst I describe, doesn't even scratch the surface of how deeply broken and wounded I was from the stranglehold unstoppable pain had on my life. Christ navigated me through all my rage and volatile outbursts in those first couple years after my forced medical leave of absence from my career, through repeated trips to the pits of deep despair, as well as through the normal wear and tear to my psyche, dealing with my roller coaster of emotions, hitting highs and lows, and everything in between, all interchanging at sometimes breakneck speeds within any hour or day or moment.

I've said before, and I'll say again, that chronic pain is the great equalizer in life. Pain doesn't care who you are, how much money you have, or how well you took care of yourself because it has the same impact on everyone. Like a living, breathing entity, pain releases its soul-leaching power, weaving an inescapable shattered and splintered path of destruction through your body and mind until all that remains is the matchstick, looking wreckage like a tornado leaves behind. The Lord gave me homeschooling as a tool to help me navigate the treacherous waters ahead. I didn't know that yet. I was in the early years of my unexpected odyssey. I didn't know what was coming. I just knew the Lord unquestionably directed me to take this next step into the seemingly insurmountable task of homeschooling.

Yes, the pain was ever present and ever oppressive. How did I homeschool? Pure faith, Christ's strength. Period. My ability to accomplish this feat is otherwise inexplicable. Let's take a peek behind our little academy. I opened with the goal of a maximum of two scheduled hours of learning time. Eventually, the time grew to four prescheduled hours.

I taught at the picnic table Al built for us on our back patio, lying in bed, sitting on the couch, sometimes dividing up those hours instead of consecutively, and I even relied on my son to handle some of the reading normally assigned to me because my eyes couldn't focus well enough or my mind couldn't stay alert enough. As soon as I completed school for the day, my whole body visibly shook, vibration-like, due to the exertion I expended, struggling through our lesson time. All I could accomplish was grabbing an apple and a small block of cheese, taking one or two bites of each while beelining for the spare back bedroom.

Immediately upon entering that back bedroom, I put my food down and collapsed into the bed in a bizarre half-awake state. I could hear the loud whispering outside the door and Al shooing the kids away so I could rest. It was like sleep paralysis; I could hear but I couldn't move, not without extreme mental exertion and mental gymnastics to will my physical body into compliance.

Christ alone carried me through that season in my life. How else, but for Christ, was I able to keep going? Self-will only ever takes us so far before we stumble, falter, and give up. I could conjure up on my own enough rational, reasonable, and logical reasons to stop teaching at home without homeschooling itself, feeling like a thorn in the flesh that could be pulled, instantly relieving the physical detriment to me (including pain and fatigue to the point of nonfunctioning).

Christ knew how difficult this task would be even in 100 percent perfect health, let alone while battling against the infamous four-star general, general pain, and all his minions. Christ knew I needed something more to help prevail against the relentless onslaught of those destroyer-type demon arrows doused in pain, doubt, self-pity, despondency, despair, exhaustion, indignation, fear, and other nefarious dark destroyers. Guided weapons of destruction strategically aimed at puncturing every millimeter of my body and my mind to deflate God's purpose for me and to send me retreating from Christ's call.

However, Christ was also strategizing. Christ orchestrated in advance what he needed me to do—homeschooling—so I was properly prepped for my future. Instead of this task feeling like a millstone around my neck, Christ wielded homeschooling as a shield, arming me with what I needed to deflect this intended rain of death by a thousand cuts. I still had the pain. Christ didn't remove my physical misery, instead he weaponized me. He was giving me incentive to keep fighting.

Christ had purposely used very powerful events in my life to create an unshakable conviction in me about educating our kids at home for just a time as this. No, let me rephrase that, I *know* he called me to homeschool. And if he called me to do it, then he would help me to accomplish it. Every time life started tipping upside down, the kids would make me laugh or make a spontaneous connection or improve in recall ability or discover another unnamed flower, plant, tree, bug, insect or animal while walking and enjoying nature or reading together, and all other angst would melt away.

Isn't that what they say about childbirth, so painful but forgotten as soon as you're holding the baby? The mysticism behind God's design allow blessings to trump cost. He was building something eternal and much stronger, deeper faith in him. Christ was building what he needed, not what I wanted. This one step of faith to homeschool led to seven years of learning at home and untold blessings. As only God can do, the purpose behind reading the missionary book series, *Christian Heroes: Then and Now*, and the way we studied the Bible, which included direct reading as well as a Bible curriculum, "Adam to Abraham," eventually led to the revelation of a much deeper divine plan intended for my future. I'll explain more about that later.

As my pain train steadily chugged through the great land of "what's wrong?" each medication, test, scan, procedure, and rehabilitation attempt was like a new cargo box getting loaded into each "disease" car along with all the explanations, rationalizations, and plausible theories hidden inside, threatening to overload the entire train and derail my life because of the overwhelming weight caused by each addition. Never-ending pain takes everything from you and still audaciously adds new nightmares to your life. As if wreaking havoc on my entire being and sending shock waves into the lives of my friends and loved ones was not enough, chronic pain propels you into the insanity of willingly trying anything and everything suggested.

Cargo boxes were filled with prolotherapy, restoration specific chiropractic, which is incrementally moving your cervical vertebrae, kinesiology tape, acupuncturists, and the superfluous pain caused not by the needles but because of lying prone and still for so long. Usually, I was asked to lie still for about thirty minutes or more. Chiropractors, who twisted me into positions my body could barely accomplish due to the stiffness and pain, snapped and cracked my neck and back with forceful motions that exacerbated my pain. Specialists tortured me with multiple useless epidural shots and facet injections, nerve tests, scans of all varieties, including full-body scans that again forced me to lie on my back for extended periods of time, all variety of medications, and the plethora of side effects, allergic and negative reactions, physical therapists, masseuses, private pay physicians, Lyme specialists, infectious disease doctors, rheumatologists, physiatrists, pain management, oncologists, hematologists, endocrinologists, gastroenterologists, and on and on the list goes.

Every day spilled blindly into the next. I moved through my day by crashing through each task straight into the next, not thinking, usually barely processing my actions. Everything became a task to get through: getting out of my pajamas or robe into clothes, taking a shower, brushing my teeth, or whatever other type of task. I quickly discarded a task if it didn't absolutely have to be done right then. Homeschooling was my energy expenditure priority for every weekday with household chores playing a close second.

Housework was divided throughout the week and only one major chore per day, if that. One day I washed one or two loads of laundry. Usually, I couldn't fold and put away all the clothes in the same day either. On another day, I cleaned our sinks, but the bathtub and shower were saved for yet another day. Mopping the floors had to be completed by my husband because the partially stooping, back-and-forth movement, and the exertion skyrocketed my pain so quickly and so high, I avoided it altogether. I couldn't cook an entire meal anymore without needing rest or help from someone. Everything was a battle. Even going to the bathroom became a half-day event because enemas became the only way that I could have a bowel movement. I'm not even joking.

Soon, my cargo containers were spilling over from repeated courses of action and the variety of types of treating physicians. I don't know why I was seeing any of these torture artists or doing any of the masochistic treatments anymore. I needed multiple units of additional railcars just to carry the burdensome load caused by trying to fill opioid prescriptions and the fallout from consuming opioids. Ingesting opioids led to constipation, lack of appetite, nausea, cramping, gas, diarrhea, laxatives, stool softeners, saltwater and coffee enemas, hospitalizations, an ambulance ride one Thanksgiving Day, arguments with insurance companies and pharmacists, even edicts coming from the Drug Enforcement Agency.

Most people have no comprehension of what the true opioid crisis is really all about, how severely harmed patients with genuine pain are when some phantom in the sky makes purely political decisions for purely political reasons. What was always professed to be the concern: pill mills, abuse, bad doctors. Weren't all those issues already covered by the then-existing law as well as enforcement from multiple law and government agencies galore?

I *had* to sign contracts with pain managements doctors promising not to doctor shop or pharmacy shop so as not to risk being dumped by my doctor and permanently labeled a drug seeker, contracts based on the new law stating I somehow no longer had constitutional protection against unreasonable search and seizure or the privacy of my own medical records without the need for court action, formal investigation, or probable cause. How is that possible in this country?

A pharmacist's license became subject to disciplinary action if they didn't follow all the new DEA guidelines. Some "genius" decided that a specific predetermined number of pills could be distributed per day based on current usage and current clients. Crickets should be chirping right now to highlight the confounding and illogical rationalization involved. Seriously, current patient needs never change, and new legitimate patients never get added in any given day?

I'm not supposed to pharmacy shop however, what else can you do when one pharmacy says we're out or we don't have enough to fill the complete prescription? Pharmacists were prohibited from partially filling a narcotic; it's the exact amount or nothing. Sometimes it might take three days for that specific narcotic to come in to their store. What am I supposed to do then? It was a regular monthly occurrence to have to try four to six pharmacy locations, including traveling outside my resident county and/or different corporate pharmacies, just to get my one narcotic prescription filled.

There were more rules. Narcotics could only be filled within the seventy-two-hour window prior to the thirtieth day of my monthly prescription. So if you have to wait or travel to various places, you lose time just trying to get it filled. Understand that even my pain management appointments had to be made within that same seventy-two-hour window. Then you leave the office and try your luck with the pharmacy, and maybe you have only a twenty-four-hour window before the last pill is gone from your bottle, and you have *no* assurance it can be filled within twenty-four hours.

Using the same narcotic I had been on for six years, prescribed by the same physician, visiting the same primary pharmacy, nevertheless the pharmacist started questioning me as to why I was on the medication. The pharmacist asked me, "Was this a new medication for me?" *I* had to tell *them* to check the computer again because it'd been years. One pharmacist refused to fill my prescription, with twenty-four hours left, because she insisted the thirtieth calendar day inexplicably didn't fall on the thirtieth day.

You count thirty days from when last refilled. The previous month had thirty-one calendar days, so the thirtieth day was one day earlier. I mean, all they had to do was run the scrip through the insurance, and the computer would flag if it was within proper fill time or not. Apparently, this was too much for her, and she simply insisted the scrip was too early to be filled. She even refused to count it out on a calendar. Don't forget, I was supposed to get a seventy-two-hour window. I can't make this stuff up. Truth really is stranger than fiction.

You should've seen the look on the face of the pharmacist with another company when I told him what happened. I know he didn't really believe me until he called that pharmacy to "unlock" the prescription so he could fill it. I heard him question why it didn't get filled by them. He looked at me afterward and said, "You're right, they just won't fill it when they could have." He apologized to me for *her* behavior.

Now I was hassled by pharmacists who were telling me they couldn't fill narcotics prior to a twenty-four-hour window, contrary to law, or they insisted I had to provide my exact diagnosis and reason to be on this narcotic, or it couldn't be filled. Of course, upon further questioning, I learned, in each instance, these were new *internal* policies for that individual pharmacy because of *their* corporate problems with DEA raids.

How unconscionable are those type of policies—a policy that dictates it *won't* be filled, even though it could be legally filled, *with* full knowledge that real physical harm and/or death can occur when a long-term opioid consumer on a very powerful narcotic abruptly stops? Most absurdly, all these rules on narcotics that place a patient at risk but any adult over eighteen can walk into that pharmacy and pick up *my* narcotic prescription for me. Trust me, I asked. It's laughable if the consequences weren't so dire. How do I keep bearing up? How do I keep rising out of the abyss?

The abyss was revealing the true nature of its depth and darkness. Withdrawal waltzed back into my life. All this "care" and attention given to cumbersome rules and regulations meant to curb and discourage the prescribing of opioids while adding unnecessary hurdles for those with chronic pain issues. For example, all those rules didn't prevent my doctor from making a typo in his prescription that prevented me from it getting filled.

The pharmacist knew what it meant to say because all the others were written the correct way, but this one made the quantity too high for the daily dose. Remember the timelines I was under to get a prescription filled. Well, it was a Friday. I was down to my last day of my thirty-day supply. My doctor left early, and they had no on-call doctor. Unbelievable, right?

Friday came and went, and there was no response from my doctor's office regarding the correction of my Dilaudid refill, even knowing that day, Friday, was my last day of pills. Sleep that night was impossible. I writhed in bed, tossing and turning, unable to stay prone, and barely capable of standing or walking for a few minutes at a time, up and down and rolling all around, all night, pleading and praying to the Lord for rest, peace, comfort, anything, to make it through the night. I convinced myself, surely, I had to hear from someone by Saturday morning. After all, an on-call doctor was always supposed to be available, at the very least, someone from his office, to reach Dr. N in case of an emergency. How did this not qualify as an emergency?

Alarmed by watching me decline into withdrawal, by midmorning on Saturday, Al contacted a friend in the medical field and asked if there was anyone he knew that might help us once the situation was explained. Astoundingly, the answer eventually came back: yes! By the grace of God, an emergency room physician in a nearby town would meet with me.

The physician was able to verify my prescription snafu from my pharmacy. He provided me an oral injection of 1mg of Dilaudid in his office and a small number of pills to cover me through Monday, so I had time to physically go to my doctor's office, if necessary, and get a corrected prescription. At this time, narcotics patients had to take a *physical* prescription form into the pharmacy in order to be filled. Someone from my doctor's office finally called on Sunday with an apology over what happened. *Apology not accepted.* The fallout for me was another free fall into withdrawal.

After this experience, my husband and I took matters into our own hands for handling my Dilaudid. What my husband didn't know at the time was I had come awfully close to shorting myself in previous months because of taking an extra pill or two, over the prescribed daily total, on a given day. Since my monthly required doctor's appointment with pain management had to be set within the seventy-two hours prior to the end of the previous thirty days, I had to plan to fill the prescription right after my appointment in that same day. Therefore, I always knew how many pills I would have left on the day I was attempting to refill them (i.e., the day of my monthly doctor's appointment).

While I could never guarantee I would receive my narcotics on the same day I submitted the prescription, I knew what I had left so

I knew how many extras I could take while still covering until my next doctor's appointment. While I admitted to Al I did this, I didn't admit how often I was taking extra medication. In fact, that is how we came up with our two-part plan.

Since I admitted I was holding aside a certain number of pills to use as extras for those especially heinous days and in light of our withdrawal nightmares, our plan placed Al as gatekeeper over my narcotics. First, instead of taking my pills directly out of the bottle, my husband placed my medication into a weekly pill holder and kept the remaining balance in a small safe until next time.

Second, we counted out a few pills from each thirty-day supply and began to keep an emergency stash, which was again placed inside the safe. My husband maintained the key to the safe. Never again did either of us want to risk a problem with filling narcotics. This well-meaning arrangement led to problems of a different nature later on but had the interim mollifying effect of stemming the fear these additional out-of-our-control problems generated for us by others.

All this, all this extra crushing weight and burden, placed upon an already compromised, suffering, and barely ambulatory human being simply trying to follow doctor's orders *for the virtually exclusive medical remedy offered for chronic pain by the medical community*, narcotics. How did all this get missed in the hysteria over opioid abuse and misuse? I was fighting every minute of every day to not give up or give in to the pain, depression, and fear, and now I was fighting corporations and doctor's offices? My railway containers began spilling out their contents because there was no more room, or so I believed. My journey wasn't close to over yet.

How can this be my life, Lord? Is the Lord as tired of hearing that as I am of repeating it? I wonder silently. As the years blurred by, I functioned in survival mode. I focused only on the day in front of me. My constant prayer was to have the strength and energy to do what the Lord needed me to do in each day. I stopped thinking of a future. I had no goals of any kind anymore except to get done only whatever was absolutely necessary to do; everything else was pushed to another day. I pushed myself to homeschool for some length of time every day, but I wouldn't shower every day. I pushed to clean up the kitchen or do laundry, but I resisted rest. Every morning was a battle to get out of bed, like hours-long battles. So when I finally got moving, I didn't want to rest again because I knew it'd be ten times harder to get back up again. I wanted to feel useful to my family. I wanted to feel as if I contributed something to the family.

I used to have dreams of my children working in my law office, to teach them basic skills they would use in their own futures as well as to witness what Christ was doing in our lives. Now I was worried. Would I be around to watch them grow up? What did they see in me now, and how could I best help them in light of my current depleted condition? Did they see joy or misery in me? Did my facial expressions, or lack thereof, and my deeds and actions reflect Christ can be trusted through the storms or being left to your own devices? All day long, every minute, I was fighting my own mind, the negative thoughts and outlook, the futility of desperately using my "tasks" in a feeble attempt to redirect my mental energy away from the body blows of pain and why I couldn't seem to lower the pain to a more manageable level. I must be doing something wrong somehow.

For years now, my husband had been my caretaker and the primary driver for our family. I had willingly relinquished control of driving to appointments, making the appointments, researching new options and my weekly medication supply, but I was resentful at the same time. The resentment was actually directed at myself, my inability to care for myself in such simple ways anymore. Why couldn't I handle my own medication anymore? How did a highly educated, capable, intelligent woman become so infant-like in so many ways?

I had almost burned down our house because I left a pot on the stove. Of course, the pot began to melt, sent black smoke billowing through our kitchen, and set off the fire alarm. I didn't even realize I had fallen asleep until *awakened* by the alarm. My mind registered what I was hearing, the air smelled acrid, and sheer terror struck as I realized I must have left the stove on, and the kids were in the house. I stumbled out of bed and into the kitchen, swearing and cursing at my stupidity. My thoughts racing, *I could've killed my family. What if I hadn't woken up? How would I explain this to anyone?* I had taken a sleep medication but thought I would take care of something really quick, and then I woke up to an alarm. How terrifying is that feeling? I had no control over what was happening to me. How out of character and irresponsible this behavior made me feel.

Who was I, and what was happening to me? My husband would ask me to do one thing, say a phone call to a doctor's appointment, even the question I needed to ask, and I'd forget. I didn't just forget to make the call, I'd utterly forget he asked me to do anything at all. Day after day, for years, this was my life. I hated feeling out of control. That was not me. I'm not reckless. I'm not stupid. But I was not the same person anymore; I just hadn't faced up to that truth yet.

Then came the day of my great safe break. My uncharacteristic behavior was getting ready to hit "meet Mrs. Hyde" status. My prison was the four walls of my home. It was all I see all day, virtually every day for years now. Usually, I never left our property except if I had an appointment or an activity related to the kids when either Al was at work or someone else couldn't come pick the kids up. One night, in the middle of the night, I was up pacing and lecturing the Lord about how exhausted I was. "What's the matter with me? How am I supposed to keep just dealing with this horror inside my body and mind? This pain is killing me, Lord!"

Panic and mania were rising. *I must have relief. I won't make one more minute.* Al was at work, so I couldn't ask him to get me more medication, knowing fully well pride would've prevented me from asking Al for more even if I could. In this pacing rant, I suddenly found myself in my husband's closet, staring at the safe. I don't remember a thought or a decision involved, just primal response. That's exactly what it felt like to me.

Hunting and searching for the key to the safe, I tore through my husband's stacks of work shirts and shorts, pockets of jackets, and any other logical hiding spot inside his closet. My body was screaming at me. I felt hot, like my skin would just melt off my body from the intensity of the pain. Tears were streaming down my face. And while still looking through the closet, I was yelling at myself, "What are you doing? Get out of this closet right now. This is crazy. And what would Al say?"

I didn't find the key in the first attempt. Discovering the location of the key became another obsessive task to me. It was something I could do to make me feel some degree of control. Why didn't I fess this behavior up to Al? Pride and control. I had a degree of resentment that Al had guardianship over something so important to my own well-being. Al became one more person I had to explain myself to justify my true need for more, or so the tape recorder in my brain kept repeating.

Al usually could tell when I needed more, and he'd offer it up on his own, and he always told me to ask, which I had at times. But I hated how it made me feel, like I was going to "daddy" for permission. Keep in mind, this was all stuff in my head. Whenever I would finally confess how afraid I felt all the time over what was happening and hating to ask him for more medication, Al would assure me that he understood and didn't judge.

However, it did bother him, being the gatekeeper of my pills, anxiety over giving me more, and balancing those feelings along with concern and worry over not wanting me to be miserable if the extra pills would help alleviate my suffering. He had to watch me suffer every day, 24-7, for years. Having these discussions allowed me to hear and witness how deeply Al loved me by stepping into a role he didn't sign up for—playing nursemaid to his young wife.

Admitting my need for more medication was admitting I was failing at being strong enough to handle my life. Pride and guilt. Every time I had to ask Al for more, it was like rubbing salt in my wounds of self-pity over how weak and incapable I felt inside. Guilt consumed my thoughts because I couldn't stop thinking about the pain and how to improve it, how to get back to "normal." Why couldn't knowing Christ meets me in my weakness or that "his grace is sufficient" mollify these raging thoughts or diminish my physical agony? As I confessed these things to the Lord, repented to him, and studied his word, the internal beast would be tamed, and the urge faded away, only to return during my next fall into desperation. Then one night, the unimaginable happened.

Pacing, pacing, pacing, I felt like a caged animal, walking my house in the dead of night, as if my motion was capable of accomplishing what I wanted: escape. I wanted to escape my body, my thoughts…everything. I stopped. Standing stock-still, my head dropped back with my face toward the ceiling, and sobs erupted from deep within me. *What am I to do, Lord?*

Once again, I was in my husband's closet, facing that metal box, taunting me because the "solution" to my pain lay behind that locked door, and I couldn't get it. Dumbly, I research all the same stacks of clothes, jacket pockets, and various cubby holes, stopping for periods of time due to exhaustion. Upon returning a stack of clothes to its rightful place, I saw something drop past my periphery vision and heard a gentle thud and crinkle of plastic as the object hit the carpet. Instantaneously, I knew it was the key. I was actually so stunned that I might've found the key. I told myself to walk out of the closet and not even confirm what fell to the carpet. Weird, right?

Frozen to the spot for a few moments, I actually debated what to do. Finally, I did look, and I was correct; it was the key to the safe. I think I knew what it was before even looking because I was familiar with the package the key originally came in, which was an elongated, plastic, sealable-type baggie, similar to a sandwich bag. We had had this safe for a number of years that just held our valuable papers, like insurance papers, car titles, and last will and testaments.

When the object dropped past me, my internal voice said it, and I knew it to be true; it was the key. Oddly enough, I felt as if Christ extended me grace that day. I didn't feel grace to have done something deceitful, but I was nevertheless relieved because I was terrified of what was happening to my body. The discovery of that key felt like a lifeline dropped into my lap because I just wanted a reprieve from the onslaught of pain. I didn't recognize who I was anymore.

To tell or not to tell Al, that was the million-dollar question. Guilt, shame, unworthiness, and fear rushed through me over having to face this decision, after all Al had done to prove his love, compassion, and understanding by becoming my nursemaid, chauffeur, protector, researcher, scheduler, shopper, and cook. He didn't ask to be in this position; he accepted this position. How was this not a complete insult to all he'd done for me and our family?

Months slipped by, and my "monkey in the middle" mental game continued as, each day, I prayed for courage, and each day, I caved to my fears. *How angry would he be? How much damage have I done? Will he hate me, never trust me again? Who is this person I've become?* The manic behavior of this "new" foreign person emerging from within the inner recesses of my bewildered and battered human shell mystified me. Paul's words, "For I do not understand my own actions. For I do not do what I want, but I do the very thing I hate" (Romans 7:15 ESV), took on a whole new poignant meaning to me. *Yep, right there with you, Paul.*

My risk-taking wasn't complete. In the end, I allowed my fear of losing access (and therefore control) to the pills to override my fear of hurting Al, so I kept my mouth shut. Plus, I could handle it, right? I just went into the safe sometimes. I didn't take nearly as much extra pills as I could have taken, while a true statement is really rather beside the point, isn't it? This was a hazardous game I was playing against myself. I understood the risk, but I underestimated the danger as well. Don't we always? Once the last of lingering shame wafted away like a hazy memory, I returned to my staunchly determined belief I was doing the best I could—granted, again, an honest belief but shallowly rooted as I was getting ready to prove to myself.

Caught red-handed, and I still lied to his face. Somehow, neither Al nor I can specifically remember what tipped his hand to my thievery; we just remember the huge fight and my lie. To this day, I'm not sure Al believes the story of how I found the key that first time. Oddly enough, Al seemed almost more devastated I couldn't just ask him for more than the fact I took more. Don't misunderstand, he wasn't happy with me at all, but Al never blamed me for the pain or for needing more pain medication. He definitely didn't understand my behavior. Al peppered me with questions: "Why was it necessary to go behind my back? Didn't I always give you more if you needed it? Have I ever made you feel like I didn't believe you?" His questions assaulted me, leaving me naked and exposed, vulnerable and speechless.

My mind was a bubbling cauldron of confusion, desperately attempting to make sense of my own thoughts, his questions, his emotions, and my emotions. What could I say? I had no answers for him. I blubbered and stuttered, which Al interpreted as me making excuses. Maybe I was, but in my mind, I was simply trying to figure out how to stop the troubling thoughts in my brain and get something coherent to come out of my mouth.

I had no excuse, but how do I get him to understand something I don't even understand? After much angst and loss of sleep, exhausted and spent, we ended the argument for the evening by admitting the only truth we could agree on, we were never going to find a rational explanation for irrational behavior. We prayed together, pleading for renewed strength and guidance, and returned to our weekly routine of Al as gatekeeper of the narcotics. My toil and trouble on this front were to rear its ugly head again.

What we both remember most is the second time I was stone cold-busted by the proverbial begging-to-be-caught move. A year or so after the first smash and grab, I got into the safe again. By this point, Al had begun storing the marijuana he purchased inside the safe in addition to the narcotics. He provided me a small weekly personal supply of pot along with a set number of "extra" pills for breakthrough pain. He had four sealed, clear, bubble wrap-type packages with a certain amount of flower bud in each packet. Knowing I couldn't just open the seal and take out a small amount, I took one pack. Did I truly think he wouldn't notice? Not really. It was more illogical reasoning because all that mattered was settling the raging storm in my body.

Al accused me of being an addict because it was inconceivable to him that I could access the safe for pot but not also take the narcotics. I never countered this damning, spiteful slur of being called an addict because I knew he'd never believe I didn't take any narcotics, especially right after the initial blowup between us. Why should he believe me? I twice got caught breaking into the safe, and twice I lied to him about it. Miraculously enough, I actually hadn't taken any narcotics. I took a small number after my first break-in only.

My focus was on how to repair the damage to my relationship with my husband. For the first time in our marriage, Al shut me out and barely spoke to me for two to three days. We were cordial in front of the kids, no open hostility, but it felt like a heavy blanket shrouded our relationship, our emotions, and our connection. I prayed and cried. Relentlessly, I beat myself up over yet another failure of my strength and my humanity and my faith. I prayed, stayed out of Al's way while still showing a willingness to talk with him and to reconcile.

Finally, the stalemate broke, and Al extended an olive branch to me. He simply stated he hated feeling this gap between us. He loved me, and he wanted to talk about how to move forward. After more tears and more prayers, we made some more adjustments to how we handled distributing the narcotics and pot to me in an attempt to strike a better balance between both of our needs and our sense of reducing risks from anything else like this happening again.

Back on the medical front, around 2010, the caboose coupled onto my now languishing locomotive was Lyme disease, along with its accompanying multiple coinfections. This multipronged little devil made all my previous diagnoses and treatments seem like harmless child's play and sent my pain train into overdrive. The research on Lyme, the controversy surrounding reliability of tests and the appropriate course of treatment, the scandal behind the board who set the treatment standards for the entire medical community, insurance companies, and the impact of all of it on a patient already fill books and movies galore. I had more grief with doctors related to Lyme than almost any other aspect of travailing after treatment options and answers.

Among Lyme specializing physicians, the recommended course of torture treatment is long-term antibiotic use designed to specifically target the bioshield encasing the Lyme and coinfections, break it open, and then kill the adult and baby microbial death dealers. I started oral antibiotics, supplements such as Ashwagandha, and others, as well as IV chelation treatments under Dr. Kalidis. After about a year, he felt my needs exceeded his expertise and referred me to Dr. Cichon. For a period of time, I continued oral antibiotics and then moved onto IV antibiotics.

The final Lyme treatment phase, for me, was the insertion of a PICC line (peripherally inserted central catheter) into my arm before the influx of Rocephin could unleash its poisoning power inside my body. A PICC line is an outpatient procedure that uses local anesthetic and an ultrasound to locate the appropriate vein for insertion. A long, thin tube was inserted and threaded through my arm into my larger vein near my heart. Rocephin requires the use of a PICC line to make it easier to endure the long infusion time and number of times taken a day and the number of days per week. As with all procedures, it is not without risks, such as local or systemic (i.e., fatal) infection, blood clot (I have a genetic clotting condition), damage to the vein, and skin inflammation. Side effects to Rocephin include rash (I always react), diarrhea, changes to liver function, and gallbladder disease. During the procedure, I only felt pressure as the line traveled through the vein.

One of God's graces in the midst of this storm was my doctor allowed Al to give me the treatments in the comfort of our home. Al was bold enough to ask, which was another beautiful gift from God, which blessed me time and again. I did not have a supportive primary care through which I could do the treatments. Dr. Cichon was private pay, and we lived far away. His office was an hour and a half away in the city of Tampa, Florida, and I needed two doses per day, two times a week for an initial two weeks, with a follow up office appointment to decide whether or not to proceed with further treatment. Dr. Cichon used logic, took a calculated risk by helping us, and agreed because Al was a veteran firefighter/paramedic who knew how to properly care for and administer the medicine.

Deceptively attractive, textured, opaque plastic balls filled with liquid death. The Rocephin was delivered to our home, and a new low was awaiting. We developed a whole routine for the treatments. Al's firefighter schedule rotated from week to week, essentially working every third day, so we chose the days he'd be home for the next two weeks. Al rigged a hook to the headboard of our bed to help elevate the medicine ball during infusion. Afterward, I always got incredibly sleepy and usually dosed while waiting for the ball to deflate itself of the inner liquid. I remember tolerating the treatments fairly well. And upon my two week follow up, I agreed to do two more weeks of the same regimen but with the strongest and most highly corrosive antibiotics used, vancomycin.

To put this antibiotic into perspective, it was used for that terrifying skin infection, methicillin-resistant Staphylococcus aureus (MRSA), and intestinal infections. It's considered a "drug of last resort" (sciencemag.org. Superantibiotic is twenty-five thousand times more potent than its predecessor, by Robert F. Service, May 30, 2017, 3:45 p.m.). By the end of the two weeks, I finally hit a wall. I was so ill. This stuff didn't just make me sleepy, I became outright lethargic and depressed. For all the emotional deep dives I'd devolved into over the years, nothing prepared me for the sheer blackness that enshrouded me throughout these treatments.

The darkness traveled with me throughout my off-treatment days and dared to seem ever blackening as I closed in on the two-week cycle. I found myself repeating phrases with my husband like, "I have to stop," "I feel like I'm dying," "I feel saturated with poison," "I just can't take anymore!" "I'm not going to make it." But wait, there's more. What never ceased to astonish me was how another layer of misery could be added to my suffering body. Of course, I contracted an infection from the PICC line, and then I needed another antibiotic to kill that infection. It just never stopped.

What my husband never voiced to me, until just recently, was he absolutely thought I *was* dying right before his eyes. I haven't even mentioned the other dangerous medications used in conjunction with Lyme treatments, medications used in cancer patients, which stripped out the narcotics I was putting in and put me into withdrawal. Even the "natural" methods, like OncoPLEX and grape seed extract, incredibly compounded the pain and fatigue still ravaging my body and mind. Chronic illness automatically turns you into this guinea pig or experimental petri dish of "let's see if this works for you." It was miserable suffering at every turn. But God also had the perfectly shaped and placed derailers to keep my train on course and moving toward him.

On top of all that had happened, what I couldn't be prepared for was the extra wreckage dumped into the lives of everyone else who cared about me, which in turn further burdened me. Everyone who loves me became impacted by what they witnessed me go through—impacted beyond feeling bad for me and wishing it wasn't so and/or grateful it was not them suffering but actually effected their thought life, prayer life, their routines, and expectations as well.

My family and friends talked to other people, seeking names of physicians, resources, or anything that might help me. They sent me articles, advertisements, and brochures of people, places and things that might lead to relief or an answer. I was showered with the blessing of people providing me meals, watching the kids, orchestrating sleepovers for the kids, and picking them up and/or dropping them off at various places. Loved ones invested themselves in me and this season in my life.

I had reached the end of my rope. I had nothing left to fight with, and the hopelessness followed me like a dark cloud determined to drown out my faith and my life. My pain management doctor at the time finally said I needed to give consideration to a procedure to install either a pain pump or a nerve stimulator. So my only remaining solutions were to get cut open again, have foreign objects placed inside my body in order to either keep me permanently doped up, or to attach electrodes to my spinal column to disrupt pain signals and maybe still need lower-level pain medications. Nice. I just cried and cried.

Lord, can this really be all there is left? There isn't anything else out there less invasive and scary than these two devils in disguise? Al and I and many others began fervently praying for guidance. In the interim, I felt I had to at least begin the process for one of these options because of all the requirements prior to any surgery. I opted for the nerve stimulator because I adamantly refused to give up and give myself permanently over to opioids.

Now, the merry-go-round was really spinning. You're required to have a temporary nerve stimulator implanted in order to determine its effectiveness. I was hearing words and phrases like, "It might not work," "minor procedure," "unstable signal," "about a ten-year life span," and "maybe a future need to reimplant." I was utterly defeated. My husband could see it on my face, and he implored with me to at least give it consideration. I decided to simply keep stepping forward with the trial and continued to pray for Christ's guidance and direction. The whole trial process took almost a year because of insurance approvals, getting the appointments set up, and the testing period.

The curious mind is probably asking how exactly you can test run a device that is designed to be installed inside the body and attached to your spinal cord? Quite painfully, the "mini" procedure jabs holes in your back, threads electrodes inside, which are then attached alongside the spinal cord. Can I say, "Not fun." Once again, I was begrudgingly but willingly enduring tremendous additional pain in the *hopes* of "*maybe*" eliminating *some* degree of that pain… if at all.

A further delay was caused by a new product in process of being approved, which was far superior to what was currently available. It was approved by the FDA, but the hospitals refused to allow implantations to begin until they completed their own approval process. Sounds familiar? This is exactly what happened with my cervical surgery. The best option was the disc replacement, but the hospital delays dragged on so long that I finally moved forward with the fusion.

I know that first fusion experience fueled my fear over how long this silly approval was going to take. I remember praying and pleading for another option and began to feel almost grateful for all the delays. I began to feel like Christ was doing it on purpose. Christ knew, in my heart, I did *not* want to have this implant. Well, Christ *was* intervening. Christ was lining up a life-changing, tailor-made solution for me, the Pain Rehabilitation Center at the Mayo Clinic in Jacksonville, Florida.

The unraveling, my final descent into the proverbial rock bottom, occurred February 19, 2016, and I have my personal journal entry to prove it. I wrote, in part, "Shocking morning so far! I woke up and felt 8.5 easy on a pain scale. I was just consumed with pain in the muscles, pores, bones, and every other square inch of my body. Ugh! Here we go again." I was supposed to be at Tai Chi that morning.

Al was at work. Zack and Kaylee went full-time at private school they were attending that year. Pacing the house, I desperately needed and wanted to leave for my Tai Chi class, even if I just sat in a chair the whole time. The weakness was nearly overwhelming. And if I was foolish enough to try to drive the short distance to Tai Chi, did I really believe I could spare the energy needed to stay upright in any chair? What would be the point? Would I last ten minutes or the whole hour?

The point was, I knew I had to get out of the house, but I also knew it wasn't safe for me to be in a car. I was pacing, and I could feel panic rising. I laid back down and continued the debate in my mind. Would I feel strong enough to force myself to try to get to Tai Chi? This mental debate went on for hours as I waited to see if the weakness or pain would subside enough to allow me to leave my home.

I was pleading with the Lord, "I don't know how to do this anymore. I feel like I'm unraveling from the inside." I prayed, "How do I keep honoring you in this pain? How do I get out of my own head and body or feel like I can do 'normal' activity when I feel so helpless against my own body and mind? What was I going to do to function?" Zack couldn't go get Kaylee because he was in dual enrollment and had to leave the high school before Kaylee was released and head straight to the college.

With all this swirling around my mind and as my body refused to be ignored, I broke into the safe again. I discovered the key quickly by simply rechecking the places Al had previously hidden the key. As I write this, I'm amazed I never had the urge to take as much extra medication as possible—another sign of the hand of God on my life, even though I still stole and deceived and broke the trust of my husband. I usually took only what I thought was necessary to get past the immediate hurdle. This time was different.

See, the true deception is self-deception. I believed I could control the entire situation. I believed I was capable of tracking how much I consumed. But an impaired mind, by the medications and the pain, contribute to severe brain fog and memory loss. I was trying not to take more than needed. But by the end of the day, how much was that exactly? If I was going to take extra, wouldn't it have been smarter to set a specific number of pills aside and say, "This is my extra for today?"

Instead, I warred inside my own mind to simply resist as long as I could, and if I needed it, then take more. Again, how much is that by the end of a day? God burst through this particular day. I sat and tried to add it up and realized I had to have, at a minimum, doubled my prescribed daily dose. This reality rocked me to my core as the enormity of the risk I was truly placing myself under by acting this way broke through to my conscious brain.

Even more ironically, it was this mental game that spurred me to turn over my narcotics to Al in the first place. When I first went on narcotics in 2006, I followed the schedule like clockwork. After the first six months, I began shortening by an hour or half an hour in between, not for every dose, just some of them. Eventually, I was shortening the hours between consistently, then I began taking from another day's stash to get through *this* day. Yes, that meant, on another day, I might not be taking the full daily dose.

I even got to the point where, on my refill day, I might only have one or two doses to take before heading to the pharmacy to fill my new prescription, robbing Peter to pay Paul, as the saying goes. This was the routine for a decade—ten years. Why, all the machinations, pain medication, exacerbates pain, meaning it makes it worse. I didn't know that until about a decade into this nightmare. Instead, I believed, for a decade, I was losing my mind, my soul, and my body to something that was proving itself to be stronger than me, impossible to control, and unable to be stopped or improved. I was spiraling deeply and quickly by this point ever downward toward darkness. When all seemed impossible, miracles happened.

5

Refueling Station: Recovery Oasis

CHRIST USED MY wonderful, beautiful, spirit-filled sister-in-law to kick open the door to freedom from crippling pain via the pain rehabilitation program (PRC) at the Mayo Clinic in Jacksonville, Florida. She had only been married to my younger brother, Bryon, for about three years prior to my entering the program. I think we had spoken in person, maybe twice, and a sporadic number of times on the phone. But from the moment I met her, we had an instant bond and connection.

Adrianne had no long-term exposure or insight into my journey with pain other than what was shared with her by me or other family members. However, she is a podiatric surgeon, and her medical background gave her direct knowledge into the disastrous impact of long-term opioid use and simply told me, "It's time." It was through her consulting with other physicians at the Mayo Clinic in Jacksonville, even though they actually live in Georgia, that directly led to me learning about this program.

As we spoke for the first time about her truest concerns for me, she bluntly stated, "I know you know this, but there is *no* good way this ends, right? Fifteen years was long enough, too long, and it's time for it to end." Just like that. She didn't know the true depth of personal torture and fear racing through me in the month prior to that conversation. She didn't know that Al kept extra medication and pot inside a safe or that I broke into the safe more than once.

She didn't know how much extra medication I took or how deeply desperate I was becoming because I could barely allow my own brain to comprehend what I was doing, why or where these horrifying decisions would inevitably lead: overdose or death. She didn't have that advance knowledge about me, but she knew for people, patients in general, the only place permanent opioid use leads is destruction of everything in its path.

Astonishingly, she also pinpointed the emotional impact and wear and tear on Al in caring for me, in carrying the burden of wanting me better, and feeling so helpless all the time. She also expressed a fervent belief that the medical community had thus far failed me and had not identified what was actually wrong with me. Words cannot adequately express how overwhelming it was to hear all that from her, the truth of those words, and how acutely life-saving they were in that moment.

> I can still remember the sound of her voice over the phone amid the symphony of buzzing physicians around me. It was late February, perhaps around the twenty-first, and I was running around completing last-minute tasks for the board at my state medical meeting. She always has a stillness to her voice when I speak to her, but I distinctly remember the frailty, the unmarked purity in her tone that day. This woman, I call sister, was hurting and reaching her limit.
>
> I had recommended she speak (by phone) to a friend and old mentor from my residency, Dr. Volosky, an infectious disease specialist. She had been diagnosed with Lyme disease among a myriad of other ghostlike infectious and pain pathologies. My husband, her brother, gave me updates in the prior weeks of how her health was declining further after nearly fifteen years of repeated infusions, consultations, diagnoses, nar-

cotics, etc. From a physician's perspective, it was baffling to hear of all that she had endured, yet she still had some ounce of sanity.

After hearing of more recent developments in her health, I reached out to Dr. Volosky and asked that he would do me a favor and speak to my sister-in-law, who had been diagnosed with Lyme disease. I was not convinced it ever was, or at least I didn't believe it still was the original condition. He spoke to her candidly and said exactly what I suspected but could not definitively state. It didn't sound like Lyme disease. Furthermore, if it were, the treatments are only for the first six to eight weeks then considered ineffective.

The part of the story I recall best is when Rhonda told me, "I spoke to that doctor, Adrianne. He made me so upset I... I wanted to hand the phone to Al." I remember hurting for her. After more than a decade of treatment after treatments, she heard in one phone call, it was likely not the condition she believed it to be. Another winding road? Another misdiagnosis? Another dead-end.

Her voice began to crack over the phone. And like never before, I could hear anger. I knew the conversation with Dr. Volosky would be difficult for her, the implications of such a possibility...not Lyme disease. In truth, I contemplated what impact the news could bring, but I underestimated how much it would enrage her.

A nosy passerby lingered in the Marriott corridor where I stood, until I covered the phone and requested privacy as I could feel my dialogue with Rhonda was going to come to a head. Without cue, she began, "I'm just tired."

"Talk to me." I urged her to talk openly.

She started shouting over the phone. "I'm tired of everyone. They all keep trying to help me. I'm tired of being in pain, of my parents, of Al, everyone trying to help, their suggestions, ideas." She was yelling, screaming her frustrations. "No one understands what it's like. They just don't get it! I'm tired."

I asked a hard question, "Have you had suicidal thoughts? Are you there?"

"Yes."

The word rippled over the phone, and the strangest thing happened. I felt a bond between us begin to seal. Rhonda's life would forever be intertwined with mine.

"So, what are you going to do now?"

She retaliated, "What am I supposed to do? Didn't you hear me? I've done everything, and now I've been told it was for nothing! What am I supposed to do?" She was screaming so loud.

Another curious and wandering physician crept by me and witnessed my holding the phone a short distance from my ear. He also briefly witnessed my shouting back into the phone.

"I'm not your mother, your father, or your sibling. I don't have to worry about hurting your feelings! If you want to quit, *then quit!* Make a decision: Are you going to fight or just lay down? That's what you're talking about, quitting, Rhonda."

Her sobbing cut through me, and the all-too-familiar warmth preceding tears began to rise in me. My face was wet. My darling sister had broken, there in that place, on the phone. I heard it, a palpable pain. We shared it. As hurt as she was, her rage and passion quieted my fear that she had truly given up. She didn't resent her mother, father, husband, brothers…anyone really. She just wanted to know how to fight.

"I don't know where to go from here," her voice said softly.

"We are going to the Mayo Clinic in Jacksonville. You need a team of physicians. Not one."

"And what happens if they don't know what to do?"

"Then we'll keep going until someone does have an answer. But you're not alone. I'll go with you to the appointments. Just remember, you're not alone."

As I said that, I recalled C. S. Lewis's *Screwtape Letters* and the chilling truth of the enemy's strategy to isolate each of us from each other and, most of all, from our Savior. Rhonda had a choice to believe…not in me, her family, or even the Mayo Clinic. She made a perpetual decision each day after that conversation to not believe the lie that the Lord had forgotten her. More than fifteen years of pain and suffering, she was *still* willing to fight the good fight. She had no idea what the end would hold, but her pursuit of the Lord was not dependent on knowing the outcome. That is, by definition, faith.

—Adrianne Hand (sister-in-law)

My heart pounded and achingly responded to the new life her words powerfully breathed into me. With trepidation, I questioned myself and the Lord, "Was it possible? Could there still be another actual solution for me out there?" In one phone conversation with my sister-in-law, Christ took all *my* previous *years* of effort, sweat, tears, anxiety, arguments, and research, which barely moved the needle on my health, and dropped the solution he wanted into my lap.

By the end of April 2016, I had my first few appointments with various specialists at the Mayo Clinic, and Adrianne flew down to attend those appointments with me. She allowed me to lead the conversations and only asked questions as something specific arose or for clarification. By June 16, I completed additional testing and appointments with various departments, met with the chief of the Pain Management Center at the Mayo Clinic in Jacksonville, and two weeks later, I entered the pain rehabilitation program (PRC). Just like that.

It was truly miraculous. The doctor informed us the program had a two-year waiting list. But if I already knew I wanted to move forward, then he'd ask right now. I said *yes*! He left the office, and when he returned, he said, "How about in two weeks." I took it. July 1, 2016 was my first official day of their three-week program.

Let me immediately tell you, this program is *not* a drug rehab center for substance abuse. This program was designed to address chronic, as opposed to acute, medical conditions. I learned the hard way that the medical community has no clue what to do with people suffering from something chronic. PRC reminds you, and I lived it, that doctors are educated to resolve *acute* matters like setting a broken leg or surgery, following disease treatments and protocols, which, once completed, the patient is deemed healed or fixed or treated. When standard treatments don't work or when your symptoms don't fit into the textbook definitions for diagnosis, then doctors don't know what to do with you at all.

PRC espouses that once a patient reaches a chronic state, a condition called central sensitization syndrome (CSS) occurs, and the body begins to simply see whatever is wrong as "all pollution in the same river," as Dr. Sletten always says. The body doesn't care what the ailment is; it only responds to the fact that something is wrong. This is key. My body does not say to itself, "Oh, I have…so now I can't do…anymore." No, *I* repeat that to myself. *I* keep that in my head, and *I* allow it to curb my behavior and affect my mental mindset.

These are the pathways *I* authorize to fester inside and spill out all over my life.

The goal of PRC is to break all those previous physical, behavioral, emotional/mental, and chemical connections and retrain your body and brain to begin functioning better in your daily life. Dr. Sletten said that this was probably the only program where they didn't ever want to see me again because then they know they did their job.

Unbeknownst to me, Christ had been using and working through other people to lay the groundwork for me to enter this program. Our insurance, of course, couldn't guarantee what expenses would be covered until the claims were filed. So, decision time, did we move forward, trusting Christ with the details? I either stood still or stepped out. Ultimately, we stepped out in faith together, and the Lord moved in mighty ways, mountain-sized movement.

The dreaded phone call: I was hearing Al's voice, but I instinctively knew something was wrong, something about the tension resonating in the sound of his voice. I was hearing, "I fell…ladder…hospital." As the wife of a firefighter, married to someone in a high-risk profession, that dreaded phone call came with the territory. However, you aren't really ever prepared to hear your husband's been hurt. I didn't know how serious the injuries were, nor did my husband, but my stomach flopped over, and my heart almost stopped. I had never before heard such pain and fear and constraint in my husband's voice.

Around May of that year, my husband took a tumble from a fire truck ladder. When he fell, the edge of the ladder landed in the space between his shoulder and chest, causing tears in the deltoid and shoulder ligaments. There had already been so much drama, stress, and angst the twelve months leading up to entering PRC on July 1, 2016. I was taking large, regular amounts of extra medication, undergoing the nerve stimulator trial, and was battle weary from wrestling my demons of pain, fatigue, sleep deprivation, and depression. Then Al got hurt. We had to wait six weeks for the inflammation and swelling to subside before his doctor could even properly analyze the damage. Our nerves and stress level were piqued, to say the least.

Doctors examined Al, determined surgery was not necessary. However, he would have to continue his no-work status for a total of three months while he rehabbed and rested his shoulder. Christ was moving more chess pieces into place. Now, Al would be able, once again, to be by my side, free and clear of any extra thought or expense connected to him taking time off work, one less pawn on the chessboard. The Lord brought Al home early enough that he had about two months to rest and heal his shoulder so once the Lord placed me in PRC in July, Al would be capable of being with me for most of my time in the program. Al came with me to enter the program and stayed the first week. My parents stayed with me during the second week, and Al returned for the final week. The kids didn't see me until the end of the three-week program when they attended my graduation from the program.

Christ watched over my entire family. Christ graced me with having older kids so the burden of leaving them was greatly lessened for both Al and me. By then, my kids were in high school, so my son was old enough to drive his sister to her school. Additionally, both of my kids had Christ in Youth (CIY) Bible camp for the entire second week I was in Jacksonville, which allowed Al peace and comfort to be able to stay with me for two of the three weeks of the program.

Three priceless gifts we received from Adrianne and Bryon were learning about PRC, paying for a rental home for the first week of my program, and setting up a counseling session for Al.

I already described how Adrianne opened the door for PRC, but they didn't stop there. They didn't ask us our opinion; they simply set it up and told us where to go. They paid for this rental home, knowing how tough it would be to stay in a hotel for a long period of time.

They wanted us to take that first week and try to focus on being together, functioning as normal as possible, and enjoying the beauty of the home. The rental home was located on Ponte Verde, near the water, and was owned by an artist. His home was filled with paintings and sculptures, and "Mr. Old Man Stuffed Statute" thing, who guarded the top of the stairs. The place was bizarre, bold, beautiful, and tranquil. They chose to cover a portion of our out-of-pocket expenses for our stay. How awesome is that blessing.

Additionally, without anything ever being said to me or to Al, Bryon and Adrianne set up a counselor for Al the weekend I entered the program. This person was a Christian counselor, the name of whom they got from a friend of a friend. They knew how important it was for Al to have his own outlet for his role as caretaker. A care provider doesn't always see themselves as someone in need. In my husband's mind, as a firefighter, "you get called, you arrive, you do what you can, and on to the next call." He couldn't do that for me. There was no fix, no resolution or end in sight. The mental strain on him was evident by the roller coaster of emotions he underwent every day with me.

They drove Al to his appointment on a Saturday. The meeting didn't go so well for Al. In Al's words, "useless" and "whack job" were his take away. Al was upset. "I'm not crazy. I'm just overwhelmed. I know God is in control. I'm just having a hard time processing it all."

When Bryon and Adrianne picked him up, Al said, venting to them, shedding years of tears for the forty-five-minute car ride back to our rental place was the "best therapy I could've had." He felt, all he really needed was to stop holding it in and just talk it out.

He could feel the stress leave his body as he talked. Al felt helpless because "all he could do" was hold my hand, run the bath, and pray for me. He was a firefighter used to being in charge and doing what's needed in a given circumstance, but with me, he felt so hopeless and at a loss. The Lord had lessons for him too. The "fixer" had to learn to sit back and say, "God, I'm helpless. We belong to you. I'm just along for the ride." To me, "all he could do" was everything I needed to have love and hope affirmed. His actions were life giving, blessing upon blessing.

Another portion of God's miracle grace was being able to have my entire family with me when I entered the PRC program, but it was not without sacrifice by others. My parents had already dedicated an uncountable number of hours of driving almost two hours to our home, caring for our kids in our home, taking our kids on overnight trips or longer to their home, and treating Al and me to dinner dates and alone time throughout the thirteen years leading into the PRC program.

As if that wasn't enough, they sacrificed their special fiftieth wedding anniversary plans to be with Al and me at this crucial time. My parents had started planning and talking about this landmark anniversary for at least the previous year. I remember plans about a family cruise or Europe, and I remember further changes but definitely some way to commemorate this special occasion. Somewhere along the way, the discussions disappeared. Family needs were arising.

My brothers and myself, each of our families, were all under attack relationally and financially, all of us. My parents vigilantly and fervently prayed for each of us throughout our collective battles and felt compelled by the Lord to give each of us a specific amount of money. For Al and me, that amount covered our hotel stay for the remaining two weeks of the PRC program. They were blessed because they were honoring the Lord, and we were blessed because it removed one more thing to have to even think about. We had the money to cover that expense, but in God's unimaginable abundance, He gifted us with one more proof of his never-ending love and tender care for us.

I knew, each of my brothers and their personal family challenges were occurring simultaneously alongside my own but somehow didn't connect the larger spiritual warfare picture of what that means if our entire family unit is under attack. My parents were in those trenches with us relationally and financially and, above all else, prayerfully. I remember a conversation with my mom about a year later, asking what happened (I wasn't digesting the fact of where I was a year ago) to the big fiftieth, and my mom stated so matter-of-factly all that had been going on with Ron, myself, and Bryon during that time.

When my parents gave us the money, they told us why they did it, feeling led by the Lord to help each of their children in this way, at this time. Even knowing that fact, it wasn't until now, as I'm writing these words, the Lord took me deeper still. Tears are streaming down my face, I feel broken, open in overwhelming gratitude and humility, as the Lord revealed the truth that what they could've spent on their special fiftieth wedding anniversary, they spent in honor of their Lord by blessing and honoring their children. Yet my Lord was still not finished. In that storm of familial discontent and disarray for all of us, the Lord was brewing my miracle, my breakthrough—blessing upon blessing!

My cup overflows. My older brother, Ron, his wife, and youngest daughter returned from their first year of a two-year expected commitment as missionaries in Cameroon, Africa, two weeks prior to my starting date for PRC. Despite his personal and familial implosion, they traveled to Jacksonville with my parents to be with Al and me as I started the last great hope for me, PRC. We held hands in the morning, in a circle, in our hotel room, and prayed together. The tears flowed freely and lovingly. Tears are flowing now as I retell this private moment. What greater gift, and yet the Lord was not through.

Our hotel parking lot became a heavenly alter of worship to the Lord. After we prayed, we filed toward the parking lot as my brothers and parents were preparing to leave Jacksonville. We were hugging and saying goodbye to one another when my husband completely released all that was welling within him and began to weep in near uncontrollable sobs.

In his words, never before had he seen such an outpouring of love to me and to him. He couldn't wrap his head around the fact that they were truly all there purely to support and love us. They each took time off work, used their time, energy, and resources to be with us, enabling us to have no other worries, for the most part, to be together in this new phase.

What was lying in store for me with this new opportunity? The PRC program uses behavioral therapy principles strategically designed to push people toward functioning better so we can start feeling better regardless of any individual diagnoses or chronic ailment (diabetes, cancer, vertigo, severe migraines, genetic, or any other condition). Behavioral science demonstrates that it takes a minimum of twenty-one days to develop new habits. During that time period, I spent eight hours per day, five days a week in classes, learning and participating in functional stretching, physical fitness retraining, and classes on pain behaviors, nutrition, occupational therapy, stress, sleep habits, relaxation, scheduling, and other helpful topics. Over the weekends, I was expected to put into practice what I'd been learning throughout the week.

The transformation I witnessed, and later personally experienced, was truly jaw-dropping. The attendees were broken into two groups of roughly ten people, although the numbers continually fluctuated throughout the three weeks I was there. When I first joined the group, I immediately noticed some people looked like I felt: dark, hunched, down-turned mouth (or at least not smiling), while others' faces looked bright, filled with light. You could see life in their eyes, smiling and talkative.

During my first class on my first day, each person was asked to introduce themselves, state how long they had been in the program, and we could say our profession, disabled or retired, and a short bit about if the program works. At no time was a diagnosis to be mentioned or words like pain or suffering or levels of pain/symptoms scales were to be used. I should state again, not everyone in attendance had pain as an accompanying issue. In my specific class group, most did not have pain, and most were younger than me.

As the introductions rounded the table, without exception, the smiling people had been in the program for over a week or close to completing their time, and the unsmiling people were brand-new, like me, or within the first couple of days. The closer a person was to exiting the program, the more talkative, more willing to share, and unanimously championed us newbies to hold aside any doubt and trust the program to do its job. Everyone who said they had attended for more than a week gave the same message: "It works." Every veteran of the program said not to feel frustrated. The information would begin to come together and make sense, just follow what they told us to do.

The reason the information might not gel up right away is because the lectures ran on a cycle. Depending on when you entered, the program, lectures, and discussions might be about nutrition, while information on pain behaviors or CSS might still be a week away. You didn't have any way to predict what piece of information would finally start to snap things into place for you. Trust the process, they say, and they are correct. Simply put, the program works.

Dr. Sletten also asked us to honestly tell him what we thought when we first learned about the program, to which I responded, "I know most of this already. I've done most of this already. How can this program really work for me? Can it really work for me?"

Virtually, every person in the room had a similar reaction. You couldn't believe *this* program works when nothing else had, up to this point.

"It's like cake. See." How does educational material mixed with strategic physical activity within a supportive environment produce real transformation when your diagnoses have never changed? How can this program work? One of my favorite "Slettenisms" is when he compared the program to making a cake. For a cake to become a cake, each individual ingredient is necessary, must be mixed in the right proportions and in the right order, otherwise you might get something that looks like a cake but surely doesn't end up tasting like cake. Similarly, in PRC, as you learn each vital ingredient, a beautiful thing happens in the proper combining of those ingredients to produce a new, delicious and altogether entirely different creation that is far superior to all its individual parts.

A witness is worth a million words. I witnessed in others, and others witnessed in me, a physical, mental, and emotional transformation in about one week's time. Case in point, I'll call her Cherub. Cherub entered PRC shortly after me. And like me, she was subdued, quiet, with her face wearing all the misery she internalized and experienced. She described herself in the past tense, "I used to be the life of the party. I loved to laugh and used to love making people laugh." She described the active lifestyle she used to have, the places she used to go, and the things she used to do and did it with relish of life. Words and phrases echoed out of the mouths and the hearts of me and everyone else in my group. A week later, her appearance stopped me cold in the hallway.

"Oh my gosh, you're glowing! You look great, totally different from your first day here," I blurted. Cherub, broadened the smile already plastered on her face, to which she said, "I feel totally different." We just chatted and gushed about what a difference the program was making already. This is why being physically present in that room with like-minded people was crucial for the support and encouragement of each of us. You witness every improvement, every goal slowly but assuredly met, and watch hope bloom, once again, in the heart of every soul in attendance. An even deeper beauty to that encounter with Cherub was that the Lord had someone open my eyes to my own transformation, which made seeing hers so much more powerful.

Dr. Sletten and some of the nurses, in my personal check-in, collaboration time with the staff, were the most specific and elaborate with me, commenting about how radically I changed since being in the program. I knew I had changed. I could feel it. My husband noticed as well as my fellow program compatriots. But I had no way to truly appreciate what they were telling me until I saw Cherub. When I saw her, I swelled with such inexpressible joy. I was filled with such undeniable certainty. Everything had just changed. Nothing was ever going to be the same again, for all of us, in the best possible way. The Lord brought me to my deliverance, and he would carry it through to completion.

Another crucial piece of PRC is their hands-on assistance and guidance in preparing you to transition back home upon graduation. The lynchpin holding all I learned together, was the schedule, what PRC calls the two-week plan. Did your head just automatically tilt slightly to the side as you question, "A schedule? What's so important about a schedule?" I know, I know. I said the same thing. While I'll admit to being a "planner-aholic," especially during my years as an attorney, what PRC taught seemed so foreign and alien. I had never thought to schedule everything in my life.

The PRC program educated me about passive (lower exertion) and active (higher exertion) activities and why they are important to balance not just within any given day but throughout a week and the month. Balanced activities are vitally important to helping my body remain in the best position to continue to heal and to improve. I was taught how to *effectively* schedule, not just my tasks/errands, gym time, appointments, and social calendar norm but *all* of my daily activity (i.e., laundry, enjoyment reading, studying, grocery shopping, clothes shopping, nights out, my new PRC "tools," such as relaxation, breaks, morning stretches, and exercises, etc.) so that I could *strategically* swap passive and active activities throughout each day as well as throughout the week and month.

As I neared the end of the PRC program, the staff helped me put together my own schedule for those first two weeks. Yikes! It still feels strange to look back on how daunting it seemed to me at the time to implement my newly acquired scheduling skills (wish I could put an ironic/smirk face emoji here) for my first two weeks out, daunting because I kept mentally bouncing between refusing to believe *this* detailed of a schedule was *truly* necessary and knowing *exactly why* it was in fact necessary.

I mean, I *suppose* (exaggeration intended) it was my pride, but it somehow seemed so insulting that I *needed* to write down *when* I'd do the laundry because I always do it when it *needs* to be done. However, I was supposed to be retraining my brain to look at the larger weekly and monthly scope. My life is no longer about simply *"can* I do a particular thing" but about *what to do* and *when to do it* within my day and/or week in order to maintain a better balance. Compounding my wariness over my sketchy scheduling skills was the fact my reentry included an almost weekly revolving door of changing environments for my first month "out" after graduating from the program.

I would not be returning home directly after graduation as most people would be doing. Al's family had been meeting in Siesta Key around the same time every summer since they were children. Since PRC teaches you to not drop plans, just shorten the amount of time or other readjustment, we kept the plans we already had booked before PRC even materialized as a possibility for me.

My first week, we were booked to arrive in Siesta Key on Sunday, July 24, 2016, through Thursday, July 28. Week two consisted of appointments, shopping, and coordinating of school entry requirements for both kids for the new school year. Week three was the first week of school for both Zack and for Kaylee, which always brought its own flurry of more last-minute stuff to do and to buy.

This changing landscape added to my anxiety of how to predict what we'd be doing exactly during any of those weeks. However, the staff focuses you on applying the principles of what they teach versus seeking perfection in application of those principles.

Filling out the two-week schedule forced me to directly face how much I truly did remove from my life because of the pain and fatigue. I lived my life in the present, which was where God wanted me, but now it was time to march forward. What was I marching toward? PRC always suggests to at least start with finishing long set-aside "projects" (i.e., cleaning out and reorganizing the back closet or my personal closet) and long set-aside hobbies, such as painting and jewelry design.

I query why it felt so incredibly different, knowing, *in my head*, I had nothing to put in that schedule because I didn't know what passions I have or what revved me up anymore compared to now, staring at my actual, ready-to-be-filled-in two-week schedule, and it was still blank. I'm perplexed at myself for how overwhelming this schedule appears right now, perplexed because I had devised a plan of attack for this schedule. Yes, I had a plan for my scheduling. I hate that I am only now realizing, this moment, as I wrote that sentence, how ridiculous, as opposed to clever, that sounds—a plan for my schedule, hah!

The "plan" is actually one of PRC's methods for how to approach completing the two-week schedule. It seemed simple enough. First, using my pencil, I had to write in the appropriate time slot for the PRC tools necessary for my success (functional stretches, the exercise routine, breaks, and rest/meditation, etc.), then move on to reinserting whatever you definitely wanted to return to, have something you look forward to and so on through a whole list of things to consider for your schedule. Truly, it sounded so simple.

Once upon a time, thinking in an organized fashion occurred naturally, automatically, effortlessly, and seemingly without conscious thought or effort on my part. Now? Now, with downward cast eyes, the blurred gaze of indecisiveness and zero sense of future direction, the concept of natural, progressive, logical thinking seemed galaxies away. I felt small, childlike, and insecure.

With the exception of painting, there were only a few things I undoubtedly *knew* I wanted to put on my schedule: time sitting at a computer, my closet, and my half-completed jewelry projects. Each one was something I intentionally avoided or procrastinated making time for due to my pain and fatigue, but each one was also a goal already previously set by me. While it felt good to have any specific goal (any outside of clinging to God), I only felt half-hearted enthusiasm about their completion. Did it really matter to me *when* any of those "goals" I mentioned were completed or fulfilled? What in the world did I have to do with all the rest of those blank spaces?

"You don't have to fill it in just because it's a blank space," the words of my occupational therapist cut through my spaciness. Maybe they really did "get" us "type A" types (smirky face). Busted! How could she know that was exactly what I was doing? She knew before I even consciously recognized that fact. And she knew that already too. An abrupt laugh leaped out of my throat. *Ding* went the lightbulb! My brain registered; that was exactly what I was doing. I certainly understood the directions. It was not a race or a contest.

Or is it, I think half jestingly to myself. Kidding.

Beyond the blank spaces, my hesitation and consternation branched out of the realization only a few interests immediately leapt to mind at all, which, I'm not going to lie, was kind of demoralizing. I heard nothing but crickets from Christ. Dead silence. I haven't felt this kind of quiet from the Lord in many, many years. This time, I recognized the silence as that, silence—silence that whispered, "Wait, not now." Still wasn't loving the purpose for the silence but not frightened by it this time around.

The memory of the above referenced conversation with my occupational therapist still makes me laugh. How naked and exposed I felt, in those illuminating seconds from God, that I was pointlessly fretting over something he already had worked out. How my inner turmoil must have been written all over my face, like a flashing neon sign. How beautiful that she recognized in my facial expression, the same as so many faces before me, exactly what that look meant. Funny to me how every time I recall that memory, I can still sense that same twinge of chagrin that I once again became self-focused, which swirled together in genuine joy that Christ still loves me unconditionally. My twinge reminds me of how quickly I lost focus, and my task of filling out the schedule became my goal.

Without a specific direction to drift, I quickly resorted to scrutinizing myself for how many spaces were being left blank instead of praising God that he delivered me to this point. I made those empty spaces into empty, mocking eyes. Accusing, dead eyes, each one was proof I have nothing to look forward to. And if I have nothing to look forward to, then my chances for success (timely success would probably be even more accurate) are greatly inhibited. *Really? My overachiever self, you just settle down now!*

Oh, me, oh my, and I used to scoff at the behavior of those silly Old Testament Hebrews and Israelites for how quickly they forgot all God already did for them or how quickly they fell back on their own way of looking at things or living their lives. Sheesh! So, while I understood the concept of starting with what you are definite about and building the schedule from there, when it came down to it, I still wanted as many of those spaces filled in as possible. I made *filling out* as much of the schedule as possible the goal. Instead, my only concern should've been whether I was *filling it up* with what Christ directs. How quickly I faltered and forgot my God.

Without intending any gratuitous dramatic flair, irrational thinking was what follows when I allow something to overwhelm me. I allowed the idea somehow that it was really important I fill out as much of that schedule as possible. Completing that schedule was something tangible. I could see it. I could track my progress. I would know how well I was doing. Lots of Is in those sentences. Why? Where did I get this sense of overblown self-importance? Inside my own head. I was so ready for a permanent change. For me, I knew scheduling the PRC way would be enormously beneficial, and I just needed to get over myself because a schedule kept me focused.

Writing, or typing, out a daily and weekly calendar allowed me to more easily adjust my activities when unexpected things arose. My schedule became my *visual* reminder because my internal reminding and recollecting capabilities were still on the fritz. Besides, let's face it, left to my own devices, my internal competitor, automatically gravitates toward an "I bet I can get that one more thing done" type of mentality, which leads to "pushing and crashing" behavior, which leads to overloading my day, which in turn spells disaster for my pain and health.

Even up to the day I graduated from PRC, I allowed insecurity to sneak back in like a thief and beguilingly whispered, "You still don't understand the scheduling well enough. It will be so different now. You aren't strong enough to keep going. Back home, life is a living, breathing, and constantly changing thing. You won't be able to remember, let alone apply, all that PRC taught you."

Immediately, at the first letter of the first word whispered, my little insecurity demon set to work in my mind, wagging a doubting finger at me, chastising me for daring to believe I was properly equipped to handle my "return."

Why did it seem silly to refer to that crossroad moment as a returning to normal life when I did feel like a prisoner set free? My world shrank to the four walls of our home, more specifically our bedroom. My persistent intruders were dimness, depression, and distress. My testimony speaks to the truth that, despite my circumstances, I experienced real and true joy, laughter, miracles, and tears during my years of "imprisonment." For countless years, I felt shackled to my home and felt oppressed in body and mind. Now? Now I was walking into a future again—a future that might feel foreign and still appear obscure. But PRC led me to turning that proverbial "corner" in my health. I was living proof. I already *knew* I felt radically improved by surviving those horrid first three weeks so I could definitely continue to exponentially improve from here on out. Praise God, I could now see that light at the end of the tunnel.

Graduation day from the PRC finally arrived on July 22, 2016. And what a day of celebration! Al and both of the kids came with flowers in hand to pick me up and take me home. Like a giant-sized punctuation mark from Christ, on this last day of the PRC program, Al received a phone call from the nurse that my nerve stimulator procedure had finally been approved, and a surgery date could be set. My husband had the distinct honor to tell her, "Thanks but no thanks. A procedure is no longer necessary." *Woot, woot!* How is that for a hallelujah? Can I get an amen?

After Pain Rehabilitation Clinic:

"Achiever" also describes post-pain Rhonda. I held my breath and prayed constantly throughout Rhonda's ordeal with pain but especially during her twenty-one days at Mayo's Pain Rehabilitation Clinic (PRC). Would she have the mental wherewithal to see it through? All previous attempts to find a "cure" failed. Why not this one also? What would happen to Rhonda if she failed to make it through the course, through the follow-on activities? It's hard for me to describe how I felt as I waited for Rhonda to exit the elevator on the ground floor with PRC diploma in hand—the graduate! Rhonda had achieved yet another goal, a milestone accomplishment, and a turning point in her battle with pain.

As I reflect and write two and one half years after PRC, I realize, there has been a consistent stream of achievement in Rhonda's life. She never stopped achieving really. Before pain, during pain, after pain, her inner qualities—persistence and steadfastness in what matters, fueled by an ever-deepening spiritual life, persistently pursuing "her utmost for his highest"—are restoring Rhonda to the vibrant, energetic, focused, mentally and athletically fit, upbeat, organized, and structured in all-pursuits daughter I recall exercising in our living room nearly twenty-five years ago. Hallelujah!

—Ron Hand (Dad)

New Destination:
Golden Horizons

It didn't happen often. Phone calls to my sister were not a regular thing, but they were more consistent over the years. The more life I lived, the more life I was trying to live with those I loved and I knew loved me. Rhonda, my sister, was one of those people, not just because I was related by blood but because I realized we were also related by faith to a Savior and Lord. What started out as parallel lives started to intersect. Pain and suffering were the axis point.

My sensitivity to suffering was a product of personal experience. When I prayed for my sister to know healing, I learned to pray just as earnestly for her to know a steadfast love, to know though, others would disappoint, her Lord and Savior would not, to know that no matter how distant she felt from Jesus's feet, she was always welcome to turn and run and would in fact be wooed ever so gently to do so. My prayers were hesitant at times because I wasn't sure if even I believed what I was praying, petitioning, on her behalf. But at times I recall a deep sense of conviction that would roll into tears that what I most desired for her was not relief from pain but relief from doubt and unbelief.

My theology knew better than to believe that the Mayo Clinic was a savior in the existential sense. She would not find meaning from a pain management program. But she could find hope that the one step she hated to take because she didn't want another taste of disappointment, another episode of God not answering her cries, that's what I hoped for her, a glimmer of light. That's all.

I knew the rules [of PRC] too, to not ask, "How are you feeling?" The director of the program made it clear that the door that was so often opened to explore our loved one's inner world of emotion and pain was to remain shut. Be with them, engage them as people we love and adore but not as people with a pain problem. "How are you?" No, "Hey, what's happening?" No, "Hey, it's Bryon. What are you up to?" Yeah, that works. Not too informal, not an illusion to pain or emotions. I wrestled for several minutes before making the call. I thought a lot about how she would interpret what I was saying. I didn't want to be the one to derail ten years of prayers.

What I heard, after my words fell out into the phone, was the voice of history, a lost voice found again, like hearing from a friend once thought gone forever. It was my sister again. I was a bit embarrassed by my surprise. So much so that it's probably the only thing that prevented me from crying on the spot. I have a two-year-old son, and I clearly remember the first time his personality "emerged" and surprised me. I was so used to murmurs and unintelligible utterances that when his vocal cords shouted, a laugh and his eyes engaged me in a way that said, "I'm playing with you, Daddy," I stood still, shocked. And at the same time, my heart leaped as I realized, there he is, my son!

What I heard from my sister for the first time was rebirth, a clear shout for joy that said, "Here I am! You wanna play?" I hadn't heard that voice since I was in middle school, and she jested with friends in our living room. And I can say without reservation, hallelujah, she lives because he lives. What I heard was life, fullness, thankfulness, joyfulness. What I realize now was that God did not take anything away from my sister. He chose to use ten years of her life to give her what no one else could, nothing else in the world could: hope everlasting, a wellspring that never dries, and a story that never will either.

—Bryon Hand (youngest brother)

BOTH CONSTERNATION AND excitement ricocheted around inside me because I knew a new and major change in life was coming. Even better was the fact we were heading straight from Jacksonville to Sarasota, Florida. All of us genuinely enjoyed the opportunity to be with Al's siblings and their families at the gorgeous white sand beaches of Siesta Key. Both of Al's parents are now deceased, but as children, they used to stay there, and all his siblings continued with the tradition. Honestly, I felt some trepidation about the trip. But what an almost perfect picture of what Christ just walked me through. Think about it, I was leaving Jacksonville, leaving all those dark years behind me, heading toward a new destination of light, sand, and sea, a new, intensely brighter future.

I am so grateful for an infinitely patient Father God who never gives up on me. Christ wants me to know how deeply he cares for me.

He wants me to be aware and grateful for his answers and blessings. Yet I'll admit, I'm the first, if not the worst, person to impatiently fall back on my perfectionistic tendencies to just forge forward because *I* think it's taking too long to get an answer or to be free of my circumstance. Impatience is self-focused. (Why is this taking so long and how come nothing has changed yet?) Patience is Christ focused. I can be patient because I trust Christ. When I trust Christ, my heart is at rest and worry-free. It seems like such simple, logical statements but not so easy to live out. Christ continues to grow me in layers.

Awakened to my new potential future, I wanted to have specific goals and direction again, like now, right now! It was exciting to feel excited again. Christ wanted my heart above all else. He wanted all the good and the bad experiences of life to do one thing: draw me closer to him. Christ was patient with me when I was not. You see, as I mentioned earlier, I can *know* (head knowledge) every person is different and how quickly someone's symptoms and lifestyle improvements vary (blah, blah, blah) and to expect it to take a long time but still *not know* (experientially) *how long* it can truly take until I *witness* progress playing out in my own life.

Christ does know how long though. This is how Christ works in us, layer by layer. I know sometimes it *does* feel as if he just ripped off a full human skin-sized bandage from my body, all in one nasty *yank*, but *he* knew what was to come, what I needed, how quickly I needed it to be properly equipped and prepared for it. My whole life, every circumstance is my training ground.

I wanted to do everything at the speed of yesterday. *Christ knew* I just needed to focus on regaining physical, mental, and emotional strength. Christ knew it was going to be a full-time job for me to consistently stick with my PRC essentials, such as stretches, cardio, and strength exercises, breaks, relaxation, and incorporating your family into a new routine while also figuring out how to apply everything else you learned. *Christ knew* it was going to feel, to me, like I was climbing Mount Everest every day just to stay consistent with those simple tasks, plus life with a husband and late teenagers. Simple doesn't always equal easy. *Baby steps, Rhonda, first things first.*

The recovery phase: I use that word loosely and only to describe the time period itself, post-PRC, when I have to practice what they preached to me for twenty-one days. "Recovery" isn't the proper word to describe a divine transformation since, according to scripture, we are already healed, whole and complete to live a godly life through Christ's work on the cross. Holy Spirit transformation is more about a rediscovery, a coming back into alignment with whose we are and how we were created to be in and for Christ, as opposed to recuperation. Mindset is everything.

For the first three months after graduating from PRC, I put my brain on hold, prayed, "This is the day the Lord has made. Let me rejoice and be glad for it," turned on various Pitbull (yes, the singer) remixes as loud as possible, and launched into my PRC wake-up stretches and exercises. I blasted my tired, sleepy brain awake, using the music like a tool that made my heart pump and made my resistant body parts bob and sway automatically, even if the swaying only occurred inside my own head and never translated into actual dance moves.

In hindsight, this routine was an attempt to superimpose something fun and positive over the "gripe and moan" language instantaneously sent from my mind and my body upon awakening. Nip that negativity in the bud, so to speak. Once my morning routine was completed, I moved on with my scheduled day that almost always ended up looking nothing like the way it started on paper. Such is the life of one including kids and a spouse.

Around the third or fourth month, post-PRC graduation, I hit a massive wall with my recuperation. Debilitating, migrating, muscle spasms have plagued me from the beginning of this health sojourn; they decided to revisit me. I'm without anxiety, sleep, and pain medication, muscle relaxers, or marijuana since leaving PRC, so my body was still adapting. The first month after returning from Sarasota, I woke up with a gnawing knot in the dead center of my spine, which was always where my highest and most intense pain resided. I used my PRC tools of pacing, distraction, my "difficult" day plan, and forewarning my family I would need a little extra grace and space to get through my day.

I successfully pushed the panic threatening to rise within me aside for a time, as I simply tried to focus and pray my way through the spasm. Remembering that PRC encouraged us to rest spasms and to not resort to our typical pain behaviors in response to any pain or flaring symptoms, I didn't initially use Epsom salt baths, the hot tub, massagers, or any additional stretching outside my PRC morning stretch routine. I stuck to my PRC schedule. I rested and distracted myself. After almost two weeks, I finally thought the spasm was unravelling and almost gone, but it just returned with greater force in the same or a different area of my back.

This routine continued for three solid months. Already in a fragile mental state since all this post-PRC life was still brand-new, the emotional hit was probably more devastating than the bodily pain. I felt fragile and broken and scared. The doubts came flooding in. *Am I really strong enough to do this? How is this really going to work? What am I to do, Lord? How do I withstand this?* Finally, I disintegrated into tears in front of my husband because I was feeling utterly hopeless again. My husband got me a couple muscle relaxers for the day and, eventually, even provided some pot, once or twice within one particular week. The strangling spasms finally seemed to pass, and my daily routine found a new balance for about a month before the spasms returned with a vengeance. What I didn't realize was that fear was rerooting itself into my life.

It took probably close to a year of faithfully following and using all the tools I learned through PRC before I confidently accepted my new reality; steady, continued improvement was occurring. Eventually, I expanded on the PRC foundational exercises and rejoined our gym. Words can barely express what a milestone it felt like to cross the threshold of our local gym again. I never truly gave up on exercise, but I went from gym rat to avid stretcher and sometimes walker or structured exercise attempt to whatever activity I could accomplish at all within a given day. However, the largest hurdle to maintaining exercise was just that, consistency. I could never know how horrific the headaches, stiffness, heat, inflammation, or pain would feel. I could never rely on how long my stamina would maintain me during any activity I did.

The Lord didn't just deliver me to a new place in my journey with pain, but he set me on his divine path and purpose for my life—the purpose behind all this suffering. I didn't know it yet, but I was in the baby stages of what the Lord still needed to uproot in my life and the shackles that still needed to be broken before even more transformative growth and healing could occur. The Lord used a vision for my future to point me to my past. What do I mean by that? The Lord didn't just get me to a point where I could hear from him about my future but to give me the strength I was going to need to push past every limitation in order to reach for what he had next in store for me despite my past.

To assist with my physical and mental recovery, the Lord began rebuilding my spiritual fortitude by ushering in a new level of spiritual connection. Two of the most significant steps the Lord took for me was leading me to Dr. Janis Modeste and her Refocus 21 fasting program and a Wednesday women's life group. By January of 2017, I finally responded to the Lord's promptings to begin a habit of fasting and seeking him for my future. Mo Mydlo and Darlene Misciagno, two women the Lord placed in my life when I first moved to Clermont, and the Lies Women Believe study, which spurred me into homeschooling, also helped lead me to Janis.

I began noticing these Facebook ads for Refocus 21. And upon a little digging, I was stunned to find out she was a local woman with her business about fifteen minutes from my house. Through separate conversations with both Mo and Darlene, I learned they both knew Janis, had completed Refocus 21 more than once, and Mo was even a regular speaker at Janis's conferences. Unbelievable. I knew this was God's confirmation of my next step.

The fasting lead to the vision of my divine purpose: repurposing of my life, actually. The Lord made it clear I was to write, speak, and teach. I was to write the story of what he did in my life. Additionally, he unpacked a vision that my speaking, writing, and teaching was like a connected network of healing, that reached across the globe and social media, would be the tool used to build the network. The writing was easy to accept primarily because I had people telling me for years that I needed to write a book about what I was going through. I loved to write, but I never saw myself as a writer. The speaking and teaching felt logical as well due to all the years of speaking and teaching I did as a domestic violence advocate and as an attorney. The laughable part was the social media angle.

The rise of the smartphone and social media platforms, like Facebook, were in its infancy in comparison to what it is now. Facebook launched in 2004, and I stopped working in 2005. Instagram launched many years later in 2010. I didn't own a smartphone, and I didn't initially have my own Facebook account. Quite honestly, I didn't want to be found or discovered by all the people from my past or from my previous life as a lawyer.

Plus, I didn't want to be in front of a computer. Sitting in front of a computer functioned like a trigger for me. A computer was a reminder of what I no longer had, no more career and no more brain or ability to concentrate and retain information. That was my outlook at the beginning. The Lord had other plans in mind.

During my fasting time with Janis that first year in 2017, several things suddenly kicked into place. Janis asked me to speak at her women's conference to be held that summer. In preparation for that conference, she suggested I set up a website and Facebook page so people could learn more about me, write my book or a shorter e-book type version to make available as a free gift to people, as well as to prepare my talking points for the conference. Talk about feeling as if my life just accelerated from a practical standstill to full steam ahead. The Lord, knowing I would need support in this new endeavor, brought me to a wonderful group of ladies a few short months later.

The second link the Lord provided to deepen my faith, at this particular period, occurred several months after ending my fasting and consulting time with Janis. In September of that same year, Kristi, a long-time friend, invited me to check out a new group she joined, which met weekly on Wednesday mornings. My first meeting had such a profound impact on me that I wrote a several-page journal entry dated September 6, 2017, to highlight the way Christ personally met my prayers:

> I'm kinda of freaking out right now as I type this! This has been the wildest day of revelations that I hardly even know what to say first… My friend Kristi contacted me a few days ago and asked if I would be interested in a new women's group she joined. I knew nothing more than that! I didn't know any actual content and more or less assumed it was a more typical Bible study, maybe more time dedicated to learning about one another but not as a life group. I don't know why I didn't see it as a life group, which is meant to stay and grow together versus only for a set number of weeks, but I didn't. It flitted briefly through my brain but was instantaneously dismissed. I guess God wanted to show off!
>
> It is intended to be a life group! Each woman seemed so incredibly different, and I marveled, again, at how God can seemingly bring disparate people together and make something beautiful… Cindy walks up to me after the group ends and tells me what wisdom I shared and how well I spoke and that I should be a motivational speaker or something! (Okay, Lord!) We spoke for a while and the next thing she relays is that God gave her words that morning. The words were "wisdom plus knowledge," and God told her, don't forget this one, but she did until now, plus faith! She didn't say they were for me or that she felt *led* to tell me. She simply relayed those words, but those words were meant for me! I've been growing in wisdom, seeking it, and currently praying for it in relationship to these "things" God is pressing into my heart! He's such a pot stirrer. You know

what I mean? (I probably need to put a smirky emoji here, heehee!)

Knowledge, I think, because it's also what I'm seeking but more to the point it's one of the things God is pressing on me. "My people die for lack of knowledge," and God is revealing that "death" to me everywhere and in everything, including those dark corners of my mind! How desperately *all* people need a wake-up call to the lies we live under and that subconsciously, and sometimes not so much, guide our life and our decisions! This comes out second strongest in politics. The first strongest is the lack of biblical knowledge of God's people, which means is God really in charge of your life at all. I certainly had to face that question myself! I asked myself how someone would know I followed God. Would they know? Do I truly relinquish my control and my mindset, essentially setting aside self in order to truly seek biblical guidance, his guidance! Do I resort to Christ first or last when I'm deeply and emotionally invested in something?

Motivational speaker! I still can't believe she used those exact words! It's that grandiose fantasy I've had for probably my entire adult lifetime but, not necessarily, always in context to Christ or my faith. I did a lot of speaking actually through my adult life.

Do you see how the Lord showed his hand in my life? He's always working behind the scenes because I certainly don't know, in advance, the people he's influencing or the pieces he's aligning until it begins to unfold before my eyes. He knew I would need support, and he surrounded me with ladies who did just that—spiritual support and more. I spoke at Janis's conference that summer, but it was the Wednesday group women who assisted me in practical and spiritual ways with the fulfillment of the book writing and social media aspects of the ministry.

Denise had the tech savvy needed to put together my website and Facebook page and ensure they were properly linked and operational. She also explained so much to me about social media in general. Each woman in the group played a part, as we all do for one another, in spurring me on to deeper and more intimate friendships within the group, as well as with Christ, through our book studies and our discussions. Three of the ladies, Wendy, Cyndi, and Camille, became, and continue to be, particularly instrumental in praying through the writing, the ministry vision, my spiritual awakening, and my gifts.

Each of these three ladies are gifted with visions and/or dreams from the Lord. Christ used them again and again to speak prophetically into and over my life. Through our Holy Spirit connection and our prayer, the Lord accelerated my understanding and opened my eyes to the true depths of intimacy that can be reached with Christ. I was beginning to see how little I truly understood about the Holy Spirit within me. My prayer life and spiritual understanding were further deepened, transformed, and ignited in new and exciting ways through our divinely appointed partnership. The Lord was lovingly providing all I needed to fulfill his purposes in my life.

By that first summer of 2017, about a year after graduating from PRC, I spoke at Janis's women's conference. The memoir writing, blogging, Facebook posts, and other social media aspects of the ministry vision sputtered along but didn't really begin in earnest until 2018. The Lord knew a pandemic and a shutdown loomed on the near horizon, a time period the Lord used to further accelerate my spiritual and my online knowledge and growth. Each step of faith I took led to the next step or phase in either my growth or in completion of ministry tasks.

Excitement and overwhelm dominated most of 2018. I relied entirely on the Lord for how to even begin thinking about how to write about one's life and how to hone God's message for the book. I certainly knew the journey of my life. But so what? What was needed for others to see out of my life? That was the real question? I began with what I knew to do: pray and read something to help me learn ways to get started.

How do I pick which stories to tell? How do you choose the core message or theme of the book when I could see so many lessons learned over the years? I continuously prayed for the supernatural insight, wisdom, knowledge, and energy needed to complete what the Lord directed me to do. My brother, Bryon, recommended the book, *The Memoir Project* by Marion Roach Smith, to read, which led me to remember my "impossible" list.

Many years ago, I had felt compelled to write out all the moments I told the Lord, "That's impossible," or "I just don't see how '*xyz*' is going to be possible or ever work out." The Lord used that list again and again over the years as my reminders of all the Lord had already done for me in order to sustain my faith for all he would yet do in my life. I lost track of the actual physical piece of paper I used to make the list over the years until I needed it to begin the writing process for my book. I realized that I had been saying similar phrases throughout my health crises, and the "lightbulb" moment struck.

My initial attempts to relocate this list failed until April 16, 2018, when the Lord had me stumble upon my "impossible" list while looking for something else. My book writing finally had a definitive direction to move. The Lord was slow walking me into his vision for who I was to reach, how, and why. Trying to figure out the best way to utilize my new website, how to blog, what to blog about how to use Facebook groups and pages and ads and boosts was overwhelming. I felt like my head was going to explode.

Plus, I needed to think about scheduling the PRC way, otherwise I'd blow off rest and breaks and fun. I knew my tunnel vision tendencies when I worked on something. I had to figure out how to get past being triggered by sitting in front of a computer again and expecting my brain to function. My health issues quickly spiraled, greatly increasing all my symptoms of pain, fatigue. *This is too much, Lord.* Once again, I took what the Lord gave me, and I started running with it all at once.

I tried moving forward with each piece of the vision he showed me, writing my book, blogging, and sharing God's revelations to me and building an online ministry. The Lord even tossed in an unexpected opportunity to teach a Bible study class. I did what came naturally. I took each task and broke it down into workable goals. The Lord gently chastised me one morning.

I was prayerfully bellyaching to the Lord about how to balance everything so I wasn't striving in my own effort and how I wanted to rely only on his strength to accomplish what He set before me. The Lord said, "Just because I gave you a glimpse of the vision didn't mean I wanted you to run with it all at once." Do you know, I actually remember an image instantly popping into my head from the Disney movie, *Aladdin*, when Genie says the line, "Well, don't I feel sheepish."

After that insight, I slowed things down and paid more attention to my stress level and physical reactions in order to better gauge when I was outflanking the Lord. The Lord was teaching me to hear his voice and to trust his pace. Each step of obedience led to the next step to complete or to the next skill I needed, even if I didn't know I needed it yet. I was practicing pinpoint obedience, which meant I prayed specifically and whatever response I heard from the Lord, I acted on it, immediately. The Lord also directed me to stop prescheduling the writing, which was not working anyway, and simply let him lead me to what to do each day.

It was quite frustrating to a go-getter like me not having a scheduled plan for my tasks. Lacking a plan made me feel unfocused and easily distracted, like I wasn't intentionally moving forward with God's vision. I couldn't see progression as easily without it being in writing. I certainly knew I was working on stuff, but I liked having goals to work toward, and the Lord asked me to lay that control down. I didn't see I was surrendering control, in the moment, but that was what the Lord was after.

The Lord forced me so far out of my comfort zone, pursuing memoir writing and online know-how. I had no alternative but to trust him for every step, which was why it felt oddly uncomfortable. In one sense, its easier to simply follow the Lord's lead, but the awkwardness stemmed from realizing how often I defaulted to doing things my way instead of God's way. I finally recognized whenever

I pushed my energy and stamina limits or started beating myself up for missing deadlines or expectations that I arbitrarily set for myself, I had crossed over into striving in my own efforts. Simply put, I was relying on myself still and didn't fully recognize how deeply these patterns and habits were internally ingrained within me.

Three years after my miracle transition through PRC, two major things began to shift. One, I hit a plateau in noticeable, incremental improvements in my physical strength, weight loss, fatigue, and stamina. Two, the Lord asked me to make changes to how I used my time. For as slow as progress seemed to flow during the first two years after PRC, it was at least recognizable because I was adding new things into my schedule. I was doing new activities more consistently than since this whole nightmare started. During that third year in 2019, everything felt status quo, more like a continuation of what had been gained. However, coupled with that stagnation, my symptoms began to feel as they were reverting a bit. *What was I doing wrong?* was my automatic self-chastisement.

My internal language became more negative again. I caught myself falling back into "pain behaviors," like mentally dwelling on what my body and head felt like and criticizing myself with should've-could've-would've phrases. I started lying down a lot more to rest and to alleviate pain and avoided tasks until I felt better. Once again, my morning routine became a battleground just to get my body and mind moving. Basically, the Lord showed me that I took the PRC guidelines and principles and turned them into rungs on a success ladder that I was failing.

I relied on my own ability to comprehend why this seeming reversion was taking place and how to fix it. Fear surreptitiously slithered back in, causing me to doubt my genuine progress. At the time, I didn't even consider the fact I was adjusting to a new level of denying my natural inclinations and drive in order to increase my capacity to hear and to obey Christ. Was this twofold adjustment actually revealing hidden insecurities in my faith?

This increased activity was having a negative impact on my health. "Am I losing, or already lost sight of, your priorities for my life right now?" I prayed. The Lord showed me three things that needed to change immediately: stop the Wednesday group till at least the book was done, scale back my painting classes and the social media blogging and posts.

Initially, this confounded me. Give up the gifts that were most meaningful to me, especially the Wednesday group? Why?

The Lord quickly reminded me that he provided me the energy to do what he called me to do, *not* everything else I liked or even *wanted* to keep doing.

He was my priority, nothing else. His way, his timing.

Immediately, I made the changes. No surprise, but the Lord was correct to target these three things since they consumed the largest chunks of my time. I had lost sight of the Lord's priorities, which were to be writing my memoirs and teaching. Whenever push came to shove over using energy to get something done, I allowed those three areas to take priority over and above his. I didn't think I was consciously avoiding his priorities because it seemed like there was always plenty of time. I didn't work anymore.

It was easy to convince myself that I made only necessary schedule adjustments, and some were unavoidable. But a week could blitz by before I realized how much time vanished. When my physical stamina or brain capability felt on short supply, I preferred to put my energy into what I enjoyed most, the Bible study and discussion time with the Wednesday ladies or the colors and creativity when painting. However, why wasn't my default to revert to the Lord's priorities?

I think it was my way of pushing back, rebelling. *Well, wouldn't it be better to write when you don't feel pushed for time or when your head stops pounding or you feel less fatigued? I'm not supposed to push myself anymore; it's better to rest. I'm tired of feeling sick and tired.* See, how reasonable those excuses sound. However, each day I didn't write was like sending myself a mental "*loser*" reminder of why I didn't write. I didn't write many times because of the increased symptoms. Too much focus on physical symptoms led only to more negative, limiting "I can't" type of self-talk and increased frustration, which compounded my physical symptoms.

Notice the sneaky way my enemy slipped back in by trying to take the good God had given me and twisted it into a negative. I was firmly following Christ's will for my life. I knew, trying to keep up with specific tasks, consistently, would probably increase symptoms. I knew I had the PRC tools, and I knew I made tangible progress. I didn't feel frightened. I trusted the Lord had my back. But...

Without realizing it, my automatic response was to do what seemed logical, to keep going, robotically reverting to an I-can-handle-it approach. Instead, why didn't I pray, in advance of undertaking the Lord's vision, for scripture to combat the mental warfare I knew would inevitably come when the symptoms increased? Simply put, it never crossed my mind that the health issue itself, the symptoms themselves, were the proof of spiritual warfare. I saw only the impact on my life as the spiritual warfare, therefore all I needed to do was endure the trial, but this one was lasting too long.

> What I failed to realize was my doubt in *my ability* to "last" long enough was actually doubting Christ's power to change something I couldn't.

Time in this health "wildernesses" deeply tested my faith. The duration and severity of my particular horror further weakened my belief I could get through to the other side and that any good could truly be the ultimate result. Well, I believed my ultimate result would be good, but I was losing sight of how I could survive until the good showed up.

What I failed to realize was my doubt in *my ability* to "last" long enough was actually doubting Christ's power to change something I couldn't.

Even after such a miraculous deliverance to PRC, my reduced pain level, and increased overall activity, I couldn't see how to keep enduring something that still managed to consume my thoughts and compromised my daily functioning. Had I only learned to tolerate the pain better and function better? If so, wouldn't it just be a matter of time before I crashed and burned again, and all that I was doing for the Lord come to naught? So as new things were added into my schedule, I didn't think to ask him about what to prioritize. I did what came naturally; I took it all on. As far back as I could remember, I just always found a way to get everything done.

When the Lord led me away from the Wednesday group, he replaced it with a prayer partnership with Camille and Cyndi. We had each been separately called away from the group so we could be brought back together. We met weekly to pray over our families and our lives. Through our meetings, I quickly discovered I didn't really understand the Holy Spirit. They had an ability to hear from and receive visions from the Lord like nobody else I had ever met. They opened my eyes to how much deeper and more intimately Christ can be known.

I mean, I believed Holy Spirit was Christ's spirit within me. I understood his Spirit was why I could be guided by him. I knew he was a part of the Trinity. I read the scriptures on being seated with Christ in the heavenlies and that all his promises are ours now. I believed in the miraculous things done in biblical and in current days. I knew the power of Christ in my life and others. I didn't doubt the existence of Christ's supernatural power, but I certainly wasn't understanding how to personally utilize that power, to access that power for my life.

These years of pain brought this truth to the surface. The pain was a constant source of negativity. How do I fight pain supernaturally? What did that actually mean to me? I did not know how to rely on Christ's strength to fight the daily battle of pain and fatigue, let alone to endure this decade-plus health crisis. I realized, I prayed and asked Christ to give me strength but not to *be* my strength. Huge difference.

I had a superficial understanding of how the Holy Spirit worked in me and through me. I didn't view hearing from God or utilizing spiritual gifts as something to be pursued. I knew I had heard from Christ before, but I never thought to seek out how to get better at it. I assumed some people just had better or stronger gifts in those spiritual areas.

I knew to pray about issues but learned so much more about how to use prayer as an offensive weapon or how to pray the result you know the Lord wants for that problem, like peace, unity, love, forgiveness, or the removal of obstacles to Christ's will. I never connected that the reason I was to pray scripture over my life and problems was to release Christ's power *into* my life. If I truly believed the Bible, and the Bible told me his Word is alive, real, and never returned void, then that was meant literally for the here and now, for me, for every moment.

All three of us became witnesses to literal miracles and answers to prayers happening in all of our lives and our families' lives. I started writing them down in my journals. I was continually amazed at how specifically the Lord answered prayer and changed circumstances and healed. The Lord was opening my eyes to the fact I needed a new perspective on pain—His perspective.

The years 2019 and 2020 brought an explosion of new growth into my spiritual life. The Lord told me this was my gleaning time. As usual, I had no idea what the Lord truly meant by repeating that word to me until the country locked down from COVID. The Lord used that time to lead me to Pedro Adao and his 100x Acceleration Academy, which modeled a kingdom-minded framework and the training I needed for the movement vision he had given me in connection with writing this book.

Glean was the perfect word for exactly what took place. Bit by bit, I was learning and gathering up all the information I needed to move forward with writing and building online tech savviness to move the ministry forward. Then the Lord had me listen to something that ignited a spiritual transformation. He used one of Tony Evans's devotionals I found in my You Version Bible app.

I listened to a podcast clip from this Bible lesson, and it was like pieces of a puzzle suddenly fell together. The Lord took all the insights he'd been giving me, what I thought I'd learned about Christ and who I am in Christ, and rearranged all of it into a new pattern. He was preparing me to receive the yet unseen spiritual breakthrough waiting around the corner.

Spiritual self-sabotage was that new pattern. Mr. Evans's sermon was about believers who were losing heart as found in Ephesians 3:13–20 (ESV). The first statement I heard out of that audio clip was the definition for losing heart: "to become discouraged, despondent, throw in the towel, I can't take it anymore, your 'get up and go' has gotten up and gone, tired, and weary." Immediately, the words, *That's me. That's me. That's me. He's describing me to a T,* bounced around my head like a mental gymnastics act.

As he moved through these verses in Ephesians, he made a number of comparisons to electrical power. He told the story of a woman who lived in the middle of nowhere and only had kerosene lamps for light. A special effort was made to provide electricity to her house. As time went by, the city workers noticed she barely used any electricity. When a worker checked on her, she explained everything worked just fine. She turned on the electricity to light her kerosene lamps and then she turned it off. The power was there, she's wired for it, but she was not using it to its fullest capacity.

In the book of Ephesians, Paul was speaking to a group of believers who "don't have the power to make the trip, to reverse the scenario, to deal with the pain, to ascertain the answer. They feel powerless and they are losing heart." *Yep, I could relate to those sentiments.* He moved on to verse 16 where Paul continued his prayer for God to "strengthen you with power *in the inner man.*"

Next, Mr. Evans made this astonishing statement:

> The *answer* to the thing that's causing you to lose heart *is not outside of you.* We want out to escape whatever is causing the pain. That's natural. But we don't know when that will happen, and we still gotta work. We have family. How can we be who we are supposed to be if we have no power?

Are you starting to see where this was going? Every word he spoke profoundly resonated within me. I asked my own "How can I…" type of questions like, "If I have this pain until the day I die, how do I do that and still truly live my life showing your glory, honor, and praise?" It seemed incompatible to live in such agony, fighting through each day, and somehow believe that struggle demonstrated God's power. Where's the abundant life promised?

The next mental explosion came with these words: "*We make ourselves crazy because we keep wondering why things haven't changed to the external when there's been no adjustment to the internal.* There's no power, no signal." Paul wanted the inner man strengthened *so that* Christ could dwell in you, which meant you got to make Jesus at home in your life, not just access to certain rooms—the rooms you think you cleaned up or are not in such bad shape, like when we tell someone to make themselves at home. We don't actually mean go anywhere you want. We mean go to the room I cleaned up for you before you got here. *Ouch, was that what I was doing?* Had I made the resolution of the pain and removal of all symptoms into a "room" that I closed off to Christ, in essence, telling Christ he didn't know how to clean it up for me?

Tony Evans's sermon opened my eyes to how the Lord can only address what I've given him full and complete access to in my life. If I limit access *by Christ*, then I can only get limited power *from Christ*. "Limited power from Christ leads to discouragement because he's not free to roam" and do what only he can do for me. "God's after intimacy, not academics. *He expands his presence within you because he has room to roam." Mic drop.*

Why do I want Christ to roam free and unhindered within me? So that I may have strength to comprehend the breadth…length… height and depth and to know the love of Christ that surpasses knowledge, that you may be filled to all the fullness of God" (v.18–19). The Lord wasn't done opening my eyes through this sermon. As only Christ can do, using probably one of the most highly quoted verses in the Bible, he brought me some new insight: "Now to him who is able to do far more abundantly than all that we ask or think, according to the power at work within us."

Mr. Evans focused on the "he is able" aspect of that verse. He looked up all the places in the Bible that used that phrase to see what it would show us. His first example was the fiery furnace out of the book of Daniel, "Shadrach, Meshach, and Abednego answered and said to the king, 'O Nebuchadnezzar, we have no need to answer you in this matter. If this be so, our *God* whom we serve *is able* to deliver us from the burning fiery furnace, and he will deliver us out of your hand, O king.'"

As soon as I heard this Bible story, my mind buzzed with the memory of the first time the Lord highlighted that they probably felt the heat from that fire. Their clothes were burned, but they were not. The king challenged the boys and demanded they "bow or burn." The king further mocked them by stating, "You shall immediately be cast into a burning fiery furnace. And who is the god who will deliver you out of my hands?" Wasn't everything stacked against them, the ultimate impossible odds of victory?

The scriptures tell us all three boys were in agreement with their response to the king. Tony Evans summarized their response in this way: "Our God whom we serve *is able* to deliver us from your hand. I know you got the match, the furnace. We have nothing. I don't know how, when, or if he'll do it at all, but *he is able*. He is *able* to deliver you *through* the fires of life, the things that you fear will consume you." The truth hitting me was, I was facing my fiery furnace and wanted that same depth of conviction of deliverance.

As I listened, three more Bible verses came back to me that the Lord had used time and again with me over the years:

> Beloved, do not be surprised at the fiery trial when it comes upon you to test you, as though something strange were happening to you. (1 Peter 4:12)

> When you pass through the waters, I will be with you; and through the rivers, they shall not over-whelm you; when you walk through fire you shall not be burned, and the flame shall not consume you. (Isaiah 43:2 (ESV))

> We are afflicted in every way, but not crushed; perplexed, but not driven to despair; perse-cuted, but not forsaken; struck down, but not destroyed... (2 Corinthians 4:8–9)

All three of these Bible references were continual reminders to expect life to throw difficulties at you. It's not a matter of "if" but "when" the trials come. These verses spoke to the truth that you will feel the effects. Isaiah says "when" you go through those waters, so you'll get wet, right? Tossed about? Maybe panic that you just might drown? Paul used pretty dire words for what he endured for the kingdom "crushed," "perplexed," and "struck down." We know he suffered a lot.

Instead, as the years passed without significant change or resolution, I wasn't sure how to keep my head above water. When the health issues first began, I knew not to be surprised by the fiery trial, as if something unusual was happening to me. But as the years dragged on, I didn't know how to handle it. How long was this turmoil going to last? I didn't know. What I was undergoing was far beyond my ability to handle. What was I going to do now? Don't the scriptures tell us to rely on the strength of the Lord. I didn't know what it meant to rely on the strength of the Lord. I understand the concept, but what did that actually mean I needed to do, right now, for this current situation? His burden is light, right? I was dragging, kicking, and smacking my burden down the road, but it's not to be this way, right?

As Mr. Evans discussed more Bible verses, he mentioned the blind man healed by Christ, and I heard these words:

> For those of you sick, the doctors don't have a solution… I know you came to me. I know you came to church. But do you believe I'm able? Doctors have *a word, not the last word,* because he's able.

Was I believing more in the doctors to get me an answer than in the Lord's ability to counteract any diagnoses in any way he so chose?

I certainly intellectually understood why Christ "was able" to miraculously deliver me, but did I believe he actually would heal me completely, all symptomology gone? I had been feeling so defeated again, so incapable of writing and speaking or any other portion of the vision the Lord showed me. The book was taking forever, a couple of years now, and my health was the primary reason why.

Eight little words right at the end of verse 20, "according to the power at work within us…" brought the whole message home to my current reality. Mr. Evans emphasized that when you believe God is able to do abundantly, more than you can even think of, then as Daniel 11:32 (NASB 2020) tells us, "But the people *who know their God will be strong and take action.*"

I certainly felt I knew my God so why did I function as if my faith was timid, had no power to defeat this health and pain issue?

God was able to do that abundance, that more than you need, *according to the power at work within me.* Paul's talking about the kind of power that *exceeds* what I can think of to even ask the Lord to do for me, not the ordinary, routine type of prayer. This was earth shattering, "bringing heaven down from above kind" of prayer. As Tony Evans said, "I'm talking when he blows your mind. When you go, how did that happen? Where did that come from when there is *no doubt* it was from him and not due to anything to do with you and anyone else? We can't take credit for it." Unequivocally, the Lord brought me a miracle deliverance for my physical condition, but he was using this sermon to show me that I needed a spiritual transformation too.

When you lose heart, you're looking for the extraordinary to be done, but you only see everything that has already failed.

You don't know what else can be done. And that's the point. Instead of fighting to bear up better for the Lord, I was supposed to rest assured, to trust, that he absolutely was able to deliver me from my fire. My weakness, doubting I had the strength to endure, was supposed to make me excited to see how God was going to show off for me instead of to unnerve me, to cause doubt in his willingness to act.

> When you lose heart, you're looking for the extraordinary to be done, but you only see everything that has already failed.

Those last eight words were a condition to those undoubtable manifestations of Christ's presence in my life. The outer display of power is according to the inner power at work within me. "If there is no power (within), because he (Jesus) is not at home, you're not being filled to the full, there is no power without." Christ looked at the power within, what were you believing him for, *before* determining the action without (externally). In Tony Evans's words, "God isn't free to express himself at that level because the power within determines the power (displayed) without. Going further with an example of a fire hydrant, he illustrated what I was personally experiencing.

Tony recounted the time he learned from his father that a fire hydrant doesn't hold the water you see come out of it. The water itself was in a reservoir. The hydrant was simply a delivery piece, and the underground pipes, you can't even see, connect the reservoir of water to the hydrant. He then compared this to our spiritual walk. "God is the reservoir, and he is able. You are the fire hydrant, but there better be a connection to that reservoir." God won't give you more power out of his unlimited source than you can handle if it will just be wasted because you don't know how to use it.

Whether you bring the Lord a thimble, a cup, a bucket, or a tanker-sized request for blessings, the Lord will fill you up with only that much power.

Hasn't the Lord already promised me full and complete access to all of it? It's within me already, and his name is Holy Spirit.

Instantaneously, I knew I was one of those people praying for a tanker full of blessing from Christ while offering a thimbleful of belief in his power to fulfill it and then wondering why everything was blazing out of control all around me. Christ's displayed power in my life was "tied to the size of (my) belief container, which is tied to how much room (I've) given Jesus to roam and root out all things not fully surrendered to him. God was trying to take me to a new level of

> Whether you bring the Lord a thimble, a cup, a bucket, or a tanker-sized request for blessings, the Lord will fill you up with only that much power.

faith with him through this health wilderness time, but I never fully comprehended this fact until I heard this sermon.

Suddenly, I saw all my extreme emotions, like helplessness, hopelessness, and despair for what they were—an alarm. Negative emotions aren't from the Lord. Therefore, feeling these intense emotions were warning signs of my spiritual imbalance. I wasn't relying on God's strength but my own. I was committing spiritual self-sabotage—self, my mindset, my outlook, my perspective, my efforts, my logic, the things I brought with me from the outset of my battle.

I took my illness as weakness, as a defeat. I looked at taking something to relieve the pain, just the fact the pain existed at all, as "proof" I must be doing something wrong. Why, because I couldn't figure out how it got started or how to stop it? Isn't that self-reliance, not God-reliance?

I constantly berated myself for falling short on my own built-in expectations of how well I should be doing in my faith, in coping with the pain and fatigue, or in my daily accomplishments. Where were all these expectations coming from? Me. I wanted to live for Christ, but how did I do that when I didn't want this current life situation? Could I reflect Christ while still severely suffering? What does "my grace is sufficient for you" tell me about how to endure the next twenty-four hours? Those words weren't magic pixie dust that instantaneously and permanently dissolved my pain. Everything was my perspective, my viewpoint. But where was I leaving room for Christ's perspective of my situation?

I was still reacting to what was happening to me instead of standing from a position of strength in the victory already promised to me, even in this. I looked at my circumstances through my own eyes. Every door closed, every treatment or procedure attempted and failed, and every medical solution, which eluded me, became confirmation of the hopelessness of my situation. Over time, these strong emotions had grown roots, bound me up, locked me in place, and became chains to my faith and limitations I placed on God's ability to overcome the situation.

I became blind to Christ's power within me. I knew it was there. I knew all the beautiful things he'd been doing in my life and my family the whole time. I knew to pray and to seek the Lord but failed to see I didn't know how to rely on Christ's strength, and my faith just felt like it was falling short.

Those chains weren't supposed to be there if I fully trusted God to do what no one else could even conceive of in relationship to my health. God's Word said I was not to worry or be anxious. I was to trust in his faithfulness, his omnipotence, his love, and his plan for my life. I was to have joy despite my trial because I trusted he had the answers. The Bible provided countless examples of ordinary people facing insurmountable odds, and God brought deliverance in that unpredictable, unexpected, unforeseen way, just so there was no doubt he brought about the miracle.

My mindset was the equivalent of self-condemnation. I didn't believe God was condemning me because I had that down pat. I didn't focus on the true problem, not fully surrendering my health because I wasn't believing in what I didn't see yet. I turned my condemnation inward, at myself. Christ said he set me free, but I had allowed myself to be bound up, turning my walk with Christ into another list of failings on my part.

Like Elisha's servant, I had been exposed to Christ's power in my life. But when facing impossible-looking odds, I became blind to the greater power surrounding me. The king sent an army with horses and chariots to seize one man, Elisha. The servant woke up and panicked because he saw the city completely surrounded by this vast enemy army. Elisha prayed for his servant to see, and suddenly, the Lord opened the servant's eyes, and behold, he saw "the mountain was full of horses and chariots of fire all around Elisha" (2 Kings 6:17 ESV). Proper spiritual perspective changed everything.

I took my weaknesses out on myself instead of getting curious as to *why* my faith felt weak. God wasn't weak, so I shouldn't have felt powerless. But I still somehow had this default position of self-blame. Did I actually believe I could somehow live in the natural realm and simply ignore that I had the pain? Was I functioning as if "God's grace is sufficient" meant suck it up, buttercup? Wasn't Christ's whole point that it *was* impossible in the natural, which was why I needed the supernatural? Did I truly feel like I should hit this magic point, where

I was so close to God that I just ignored what was happening in my body, like flipping a switch? Poof, the pain was now ignorable.

I *was* functioning better in relationship to my pain after PRC. The Lord brought me to a place where I was more intentionally aware of the spiritual battle at work. I was praying more specifically, praying scripture over my life, and seeking direction from the Lord. The devil's whole purpose was for me to feel separated from the Lord because then I'm not doing the work of the Lord, let alone looking to Christ at all. The severity and longevity of this trial caused me to be hyper-focused on my circumstances every day instead of seeing beyond the storm and into the eyes of my Lord and Savior.

> I hadn't forgotten what the Lord had already done for me, but I didn't know how to see a future, still with pain and fatigue, that could net a different end result.

If the devil kept me focused on shame, fear, and doubt connected to my health or anything negative, then I'm not focused on Christ. I become less consciously aware of how the Lord may continue to choose to use me now. I cannot even dream of God's future possibilities if I'm still focused on the past.

After listening to Mr. Evans's sermon, I realized I was still praying in safe ways for my future, in light of what my past reflected, which was the belief that without my health being fully resolved, then I might not be able to sustain what the Lord gave me to do. Do you see how entrenched negative mindsets can be?

I hadn't forgotten what the Lord had already done for me, but I didn't know how to see a future, still with pain and fatigue, that could net a different end result.

Did I know how to believe for things I did not yet see? Who was I really relying on to change everything for me? I began to pray, "Enable me to gain a new perspective on pain" and "to wake up with something else on my mind besides the pain. Allow me to look forward more to what you have next in store and what you are asking me to do now than anything related to my past." The very next morning, I woke up with a list of things to get done for the day. I couldn't even remember the last time I went through a mental to-do checklist, and it felt amazing. God's graciousness was unending.

God showed me he could enable me to do something I never believed possible, to not have the pain command my day. Everything changed that morning. I had been placing limits on Christ. I wasn't using his power. I was fighting the war with the wrong weapons. I couldn't see how I could become that David or Moses or Abraham of faith because look at me. Who am I? I'm still broken. What did Christ see? He saw his chosen one, his equipped one, his strong one, and his masterpiece. Whose expectation am I striving to live up to when Christ tells me I am forgiven, healed, and whole in him?

As these revelations soaked in, I immediately began praying and literally visualized chains and shackles breaking off my wrists, my neck, and my feet. I felt it in my body, like actual weight being lifted off of me. It was unbelievable. I told the Lord, "I don't want to carry the burden of the pain anymore. I don't want to fight you anymore." Christ revealed to me that I'd been fighting his sovereignty. I refused to let go of the belief that somehow I could still control my circumstances or my mind or my pain.

For that matter, why did I even want to try in the first place? Christ was the only one in charge of any of those things. Christ dropped the PRC program right into my lap, the program which enabled me to be where I'm at right now. If he brought me to this point, he'd get me all the way through.

I'm the one who kept glancing back at my past, at all those "mistakes." I made expectations for myself so I could see if I was making progress mentally, physically, and spiritually. Christ saw only where He was taking me. Christ only saw the future purpose he laid out for me to fulfill. He knows I'm not perfect. These thoughts just cascaded through me.

If God already knew what I'd be struggling with, then he knew what it would take to push me through this situation. I finally recognized how much power I gave to the pain and how little power I gave to Christ. There are no limitations to God. I finally recognized what an enormous waste of time and energy it was to be frustrated or upset by the reality of my physical and mental limitations. While those limitations are real to me in the physical realm, I'm to be believing in the supernatural realm, the power of God, and he has no limits. Of course, I couldn't figure it all out. The Lord never expected me too. These are the spaces in life where the Lord can show off in those unpredictable and miraculous ways.

Instead of beating myself up for my own humanity, I should be jumping for joy that Christ was in my life. Christ knew every thought I'd ever have and still delivered me and called me into a beautiful purpose. He took my broken mess and turned it into something beautiful. He got me here. It's his work within me and through me. My own capabilities, real or perceived, are irrelevant. Christ maneuvered behind the scenes, brought all the right people into place to open up the PRC avenue for me. As I sit here today, I am grateful for a Christ who loved me so dearly that he demonstrated his undeniable presence in my life.

Obsessive thoughts of "what if" and "how come" or "should" no longer flooded my mind. I do not dwell on the pain but on following this path of writing, teaching, and healing he's placed before me. I learned to relish that no matter what he asked me to do, he would provide me the strength, stamina, and resources needed to complete the task. Today, the pain and fatigue are still present and unpredictable, but different, much less than it once was.

I do not fear the pain anymore. I don't worry about it at all. Daily, I take communion and pray a rotating set of healing prayers. I know I am healed. My symptoms will fully disappear as I continue to move forward with each step of obedience, no matter what. I am overjoyed because I know my Lord is alive, real, and personal because of what I've already experienced firsthand.

I know I can believe in what I do not yet see. He dismantled my life in order to show me I had him in my life but not over my life. He showed me my double-mindedness, that I confessed my belief but doubted in my heart. Christ needed to restructure my spiritual goggles so I could see him better. He mushed my brain, knocked out all that I built, dumped it out, and began to refill me with intimacy with him, his wonder, ignited my prayer life, and brought me every person, insight, and tool needed to move forward with my health and with his vision. I didn't see how it was all possible, but Christ knew it was, and he needed me to know it too.

Trials mold warriors, and Christ wanted me to trust him as my leader. All soldiers are trained and tested. He's already equipped me for all I will face in life, my training ground.

Christ didn't want me to keep living like a secular person with a spiritual background but as his spiritually armored warrior living in the world, doing his work.

God used a friend, Bridget Moses, to perfectly proclaim, one day, words that felt ripped from my own soul: "God has stretched me *far beyond* what I ever thought possible. He's increased my capacity for faith and for that faith to manifest. I know that he's waited until my capacity expanded enough for what's up ahead. He has a *massive* purpose for my life that needs a *massive* capacity for that faith to operate in, to move forward."

These are absolutely true words. I had to learn how to see beyond the pain train chugging through my body, trying to contain me and control me, and believe it would only end in a train wreck. Christ alone turned that train around and set it onto new tracks. I had to learn to rely on the power of Christ to do the impossible in order to fully embrace his purpose for my life. Christ taught me to see him beyond the storm so I could step past every self-imposed limitation and walk freely and fully in the purpose and power of Christ.

> Christ didn't want me to keep living like a secular person with a spiritual background but as his spiritually armored warrior living in the world, doing his work.

Sanctification is not my idea of what I want God to do for me. Sanctification is God's idea of what he wants to do for me.

—Oswald Chambers

About the Author

CHAIN-BREAKING, FAITH-JUMPING WAR-RIOR is the character Christ carved out of a shy, perpetual "new" girl persona as the daughter to a dad in the military. Her personal memoir, *Journey Derailed: Is Your Hope for Healing Tied to a Diagnosis, an Expected Outcome, a Cure, or to Christ?* tells her almost two-decade journey of unimaginable suffering from an unexpected chronic illness, which led to the dissolution of her own law firm, plunging her into a darkness she thought she would never rise above and back out into startling breakthroughs and renewal never imagined possible. She is currently living in Clermont, Florida, as a wife, a mother of two young adult children, and a kingdom entrepreneur for her Lord and Savior Jesus Christ.

To find out more about Rhonda and what the Lord has her up to, go to www.journeyderailed.com or find her on Facebook as Journey Derailed and on Instagram as @journeyderailed.